CROSS

BUDDHA

Our Amazing Journey

E. Raymond and Janet V. Rock

Contents

Chapter One

1. Lost Innocence

I glanced out the side window of the junked '37 Chevy. The old coupe had a smell about it, musty; and while it sat there quietly whispering to me of its many roads traveled, the sweet scent of summer hay and the muted, golden sunshine of those unpredictable Ohio skies etched themselves in bronze during this enchanted period of my childhood.

Gramma was making her way across the pasture, "Edward! You drive me to church," she demanded, in her thick German accent. She had Grampap's straw hat in her hand. I called back with an exuberant, "Okay!"

Mom, Dad and Grampap usually worked on Sundays, so it was a good day to sneak out to the field and race that old car around for awhile. I must have been a tolerable mechanic at ten years old to keep it running, but I never drove on a real asphalt road before.

With no brothers or sisters to keep me straight, I grew up independent as hell crossing the line between daring and recklessness every day. Gramma wasn't much better. She was a little crazy, too. She had seen it all, or most of it, during her sixty-odd years, and she used that wisdom generously to push along her audacious grandson.

Only when I looked back did I appreciate the many ways in which she challenged me. She made me test myself repeatedly and I became stronger for it, only discovering later how I would need every bit of that strength — when the journey began.

She plopped Grampap's old straw hat on my head, "To make you look older in case Harry (the local constable) sees us," and off we went with Gramma holding on for dear life to the door handle of an old Chevy with no plates. Before we knew it, I had smoothly navigated the three miles to the Catholic Church she loved, not passing one other car. I was on top of the world, soaring. Wow! I actually drove on a paved road!

Janet: "About the time that Ed was having fun driving his grandmother to church, I was being born. Life was so easy for him regardless of what he did because he had great karma.

When he was seventeen and eloping with his high school sweetheart before heading to college on a four-year football scholarship, I was seven and sadly kissing my mother goodbye for the last time.

Fast forward twenty years and my very dark nights changed into incredible sunlit mornings when I met him for the first time and his good karma began to rub off on me.

It was a strange thing. I felt as if I had known him my entire life, and he was my lifesaver."

It was the beginning of many Sunday trips Gramma and I secretly made to that little church, but then one night she unexpectedly up and died on me. They said it was a massive stroke.

I missed her a lot. She had a sense of spontaneity like nobody else in the family. Everyone else was careful, always worried about stuff, but she had guts and a way about her of never telling me things outright. She made me learn by watching her, things like; it was impossible to be careful and free at the same time, and that fear and love are like oil and water; you can't mix 'em. Something began to register then; something that watches a kid grow up but isn't exactly him. The fact, however, was that Gramma was gone, and I was on my own.

Childhood memories can be beautiful things. I vividly recall the soft petals of spring wildflowers brushing my cheek, and winter snowflakes melting on my tongue. At the time, it didn't feel childish at all; it was all so real. And oh so close to truth. Why was a snowflake so amazing to me then? Maybe it was because I was surrounded with wonderment.

Janet: "Both of us seemed to have little insights when we were kids. One time I distinctly remember thinking, "Why was I born?" My next thought was, "I didn't have to be born, but for some reason I was!" This happened when I was about nine years old and hadn't a clue about past lives, future lives or anything like that.

They say that we all have an underlying karma from past lives that nudges us in certain directions and shapes our current life, and from my perspective now, I certainly believe that to be true."

I somehow made it to eight years old and loved the ten-cent cowboy movies at that old Rialto Theatre in Johnstown, where big skies and mountains filled the screen with plots as black and white as the cowboys' hats and horses. The Glitzy Cowboys like Roy Rogers and Gene Autry weren't for me; guitars and silver pistols didn't belong out 'thar' where real men rode! I was drawn to the shy but intense cowboys like Johnny Mack Brown and Bob Steele, and whenever the bad guys did their despicable things, I would become terribly upset. I just didn't get it; how could the bad guys not understand that the world was good and that everybody in it was supposed to be trusting and truthful?

Before I knew it, I was in the middle of the Fabulous Fifties, and my dad was building a little house on farmland just south of Cleveland. It was there that I learned to drive that old Chevy and do all the neat things that kids out in the country do, like skinny-dipping in the creek, hunting, wandering the woods, sleeping in hay barns, and sled riding in the pastures.

Janet: "I met Ed when he was thirty-six, just after he left his wife and children. We had a lot in common; our Catholic background, report cards full of A's, wearing glasses, playing the clarinet in junior high and . . . spiritual genes."

Sports came easily. Fortunately, I was in a small town where there wasn't much competition that set me up for a football scholarship at Furman University in South Carolina. So that's where I now headed, with my high school sweetheart who snuck out through her bedroom window at 2:00 in the morning in that summer of high school graduation to head downstate and tie the knot with another rebel, just like her!

Before we knew what was happening, we were twenty-two years old with two kids, one on the way, and heading to San Francisco with a '57 Chevy station wagon and $400 dollars in our pockets.

Ten years later, we were a perfect family nestled in a secure career with Shell Oil. Never were there the slightest problems between any of us. No dramas, no catastrophes, just camping trips, cookouts, football games, and family vans as we transferred from the Bay Area, to Spokane and to Boise. Everything was picture-perfect. I was thirty-two with a great wife, three great kids, and a promising career.

It was while I was at Furman, back when I was eighteen, that one of my weird, spiritual genes began stirring; one of the strongest memories of my life. I distinctly recall sitting at a table in the cafeteria reading a book between classes, football practice, ROTC and my night job at a cotton mill, but can't remember the title. Anyway, it suggested that I concentrate my mind on these two words, "I AM."

Why I was so attracted to this simple exercise, or even the book, I can't fathom, but I was. I focused on "I AM" for about a minute, really concentrating hard. Nothing was there except "I AM."

I'll never forget the experience. How could I do that; stay concentrated without a single thought other than, "I AM?" My mind went through some kind of a permanent transformation right then and there.

The experience lodged itself in my mind as if a seed was planted, and looking back, a seed certainly was. At the time, I wasn't aware yet of how seeds, so tiny, can grow to create colossal epiphanies, as well as enormous complications twenty years later.

Later in my thirties, I enjoyed reading Tolkien's fantasies that moved me in strange ways and triggered something that was already going on deep inside. Not long afterwards, I found myself alienated, confused, and taking long, solitary walks. Everything around me was changing, as if it was out of control. I didn't fit in anymore. I felt as if either I had moved on and every-

5

thing else hadn't, or everything was moving on and I couldn't, as if I was a fish out of water that longed to return home but no longer knew where home was.

My family and my wonderful life surrounded me, so why did I feel so estranged? I knew nobody would understand because how could I explain something that I didn't understand myself? It's clear now what was going on, but not at the time. All I felt then was something pulling me away from everyone and everything I held dear.

Janet: "Although we both got mostly 'A's on our report cards, I was a plodder and a perfectionist having to study for hours and hours every day, while Ed never bothered with homework at all. He would finish a thirty-minute test in five minutes and then get in trouble, while I, on the other hand, would be one of the last to turn it in after checking everything numerous times, and never got in trouble!

Ed was born with a high IQ (more good karma), so he was forever questioning and weighing things, but his evaluations and interests were mostly directed internally and psychologically rather than outwardly toward ambition or money. My interests were similar because I wanted answers to life after my mom died when I was so young.

Couple all of this with a fearlessness to follow our intuitions regardless of the consequences, and you have a hint about what lay ahead for both of us."

My family, my home, my career, my bank account, my good health; these were my refuges, but a refuge is a place to hide. I couldn't see things while I was hiding down in my secure foxhole, and when I couldn't see things, no further possibilities existed.

My gramma's words came back to me, "You can't be careful and free, too," and I felt dead inside. Was I now about to sacrifice it all? For what?

My mother would tell me, "Edward, you are never satisfied," and she was right, as usual. I was never satisfied, not in my entire life. It was as if I was always running from something or toward something, certain that it was the answer, but it never was.

I would attack everything until I strangled the life out of it, using up all of its substance before tossing it aside in disgust and already in the hunt for something new. Only beginnings satisfied my creativity, never maintaining them.

Playing with my exotic foreign cars, pool tables, relationships and all the rest of it eventually just wearied me. Whatever it was that I achieved, I would eventually want it out of my life. If I couldn't get rid of it, hostility and agitation would take over with a vengeance. I just couldn't seem to trust outside stimulations because I realized that they would never last – an insight that would be later confirmed.

I became really confused whenever something nudged me in strange directions that didn't make sense whatsoever to my logical mind, such as a scary indication that nothing in life lasts. These compulsions began as small, silent urges deep in my heart, quiet and unassuming in many ways, but in other ways, extremely powerful. They were not to be ignored.

Many of these urgings were exceptionally delicate and easily overwhelmed by my intellect, but eventually I learned to choose intuition over intellect because everything that was creative and insightful seemed to come from there, even though this intuition was universes apart from any consideration of security.

At times, I wondered if my grandmother was whispering to me from her grave, "Follow your heart, Edward." Unfortunately, instead of following my true heart, I often followed my passions with their urges taking me in directions that would cause pain to many others; people who would never understand. How could they? I couldn't understand it myself, as I was about to walk away from everything I held dear.

Chapter Two

2. Unanswered Questions

After leaving my family, my career, my home, and a life that I was familiar with, I knocked around for awhile ending up in a lonely apartment building back in Cleveland, and confused as ever. One day, I burst into the laundry room across the hall carrying three baskets of dirty clothes, and frightened a young woman half to death. This awkward meeting of a woman in curlers and me a wild man was to eventually lead to auspicious things, but neither of us had a clue at the time.

Our backgrounds were alike in many ways, yet so different. Janet was twenty-six, I was thirty-six, and both born under the sign of the crab. We both grew up in the Cleveland area, and had a Catholic background.

Janet: "I was the youngest of five siblings; Ed was an only child, and while he attended Catholic school for a year or two, I spent twelve years there.

My mother wanted to be a nun, same as Ed's, but before my mother had a chance to fulfill her dreams, her parents suddenly died a few months apart. Her aspirations were dashed. Since she was the oldest of seven younger brothers and sisters, she had no choice but to take over the entire household at the tender age of eighteen. She eventually married and produced five offspring, with me being the baby of the family.

My early years were hazy, maybe because I was only seven when my mom, after suffering for a long time, died of uterine cancer. Only years later did my second oldest sister tell me things about my mom during this time that I never knew.

Our mom had gone to a few doctors who confirmed that she had only a few months to live, and she was really upset. However, she had a strong heart and a lot of hope and never complained, but wondered what she ever did to deserve so much pain.

Although she could not understand why her kids weren't going to have a mother because she didn't have one for long either, her mind was eased knowing that she tried to teach her five children everything she could while raising them.

She unbelievably managed to hang on for three painful years, desperately trying to take care of her young family, but it was hard. My sister divulged times when our mother would go into our tiny utility room in our small house and pound the floor with a hammer so that no one could hear her screams when the pain became unbearable.

I recall hiding in a closet sometimes when I was little, but why, I couldn't remember as though the reason was so horrible it permanently erased itself from my memory. Some things, however, I never forgot, like the day a favorite aunt took me on her lap and told me that my mom had died.

It was December 23. I was so looking forward to the few presents waiting for me under a small Christmas tree. My Christmases were never the same again.

At the funeral, I was told to kiss my mom goodbye. I kissed her forehead, expecting it to be warm and soft as I remembered, but it was cold and hard like a marble statue – and it shocked me. That was the moment I began to question life. I had heard about death, but now death touched my seven-year-old heart, and I was shaken. I could not understand how God worked. I needed her so much at this young age.

My two older sisters took over the cooking and cleaning, caring for all of us, but it was difficult. There was little money and the place was small and noisy. My father's remarrying and moving to another house compounded a difficult situation, and his drinking, which had always complicated our lives, continued, even though he never missed a day of work.

Eventually, my oldest brother married and my two sisters moved out on their own, which left me living in a strange house with my dad and stepmother, who worked nights, and my second oldest teenage brother who was constantly on the go. This left me by myself much of the time, making it a very lonely period in my life.

I remembered some good times, too. My dad was nice to me, occasionally taking me out of the city to Byesville, the small, southern Ohio town where he grew up. I always had great fun with my only grandmother, along with my aunts, uncles, and cousins, but whenever I showed Ed my family photographs, he quickly pointed out that everyone was smiling but me, in every last one of them.

My dad did the best he could; going through the motions like any man does when picking up the pieces, and saved enough money to send me, his baby, to Bowling Green State University. He was so proud of that, but when he was fifty-six, he died of a massive heart attack. It seemed as if everything that I had left in the world was being slowly taken away.

His death was easier for me to accept than my mom's was. It might have been because that first experience of death hit me so hard that there wasn't much left. Or, perhaps I was older now. The only comforting aspect was that I no longer had to worry about his alcoholism and or watch him suffer the way he did.

Being on my own at a young age was difficult for me. I recall visiting a local Catholic church, often alone, sometimes in the mornings, sometimes in the afternoons. I was sensitive, very confused, and extremely depressed. I pleaded for answers, prayed for them . . . but none ever came. I considered suicide once or twice, but just couldn't do it; it didn't feel right.

I thought about what to do with my life and thought about becoming a teacher, a nun, or a flight attendant because I wanted to travel. Missionary work crossed my mind as well, but nobody was there to encourage me with my aspirations. Frankly, I was a little scared and eventually decided to stay close to home and become a schoolteacher.

Studying never came easy to me. I was a slow, steady turtle, determined and staying up late almost every night trying to memorize things that other kids picked up easily. Whenever my mind was contacted by anything, there was a pause that other people didn't seem to have, and as I desperately tried to retain what was said a moment ago, I would miss what was being said presently. As a result, my nickname in college was 'Spacey," however, I was intuitive, sensitive, and wise in other ways and no matter the hardships, I persevered and did things right. That's how I was – a turtle –while Ed was a rabbit.

It was an incredible struggle, but I somehow graduated from Bowling Green State University in Ohio and fulfilled my dream by teaching fourth grade at a

Catholic elementary school close to my old high school. I didn't stray too far from home.

As it turned out, however, my teaching career never got off the ground and my bad luck continued; nothing ever worked out for me even though I gave my all in everything I did.

The Catholic school loaded each of us teachers down with over forty kids, but even that wasn't the problem. I somehow handled it by staying up late every night, trying to prepare thoughtful lessons to keep the kids involved. The kids loved me. I wasn't the problem. The problem was that the Church decided to replace all the lay teachers with nuns, and I found myself out of a job.

Since I wasn't confident enough to tackle a public school teaching position, I tried my luck at accounting, landing a job with a large corporation in Cleveland. I did well in accounting, since my strengths were steadiness, reliability, and accuracy, especially when my mind had time to digest the material at my own pace, but cliques and personality conflicts bothered me and since I was quiet and sensitive, the backstabbing became so bad that I soon became despondent. I wondered if something wasn't wrong with me. Why were things always so difficult?

Ed and I became aware of our common sensitivities soon after we began seeing each other, and after a month or two, he became my closest and best friend ever. Although it was a strange and amazing feeling, I was still hesitant about him. He was going through a divorce and still married with three children, and I wasn't at all certain that I should get involved. The Church would not approve of this. Despite these reservations, I went with my gut feeling and disregarded

13

the Church's doctrines, which was a difficult thing for me to do.

After we had been going together for about a year and his divorce was final, I mentioned one day that a dream of mine was to go out west."

So, Janet wanted to move out west. Great! This was right up my restless alley – a new beginning!

Before you could say '*Phoenix,*' we were on our way to Arizona with a U-Haul, my smoking credit cards and an incorrigible, reckless attitude. I was still out for myself and a good time, or thought I was. It's peculiar how two people can be drawn into unknown immensities while still acting out old karma.

Not long after our dash out west, bill collectors got serious about my wild spending by harassing me at work and making my life as miserable as only they knew how. It ended up being a battle of wits, with me stubbornly determined not to pay them a damn nickel, and the bill collectors repossessing my car. It wasn't long before I was predictably looking for a place in which to disappear.

There were some questions that I had wanted answered as well. Since my shallow Catholic background was steeped in useless mystery, mystiques, and miracles where I was never exposed to Catholicism's deeper aspects, such as contemplative prayer and meditation, either the religion I was born into was failing me, or I was failing it.

I had been doing some casual reading about Eastern religions, particularly Buddhism that seemed to be on the same page as my organized German heritage with its clear, concise, open honesty. So one day I decided it would be a good idea to go off alone, like the

Buddha did, and maybe, more importantly, to a place where my bill collectors couldn't find me.

One morning I loaded all my stuff into a couple of huge suitcases and a backpack, and wrote a short note to Janet, who had already left for her furniture sales job in Phoenix, explaining that I would be gone for awhile.

I then took a moment to look around at the stuff we accumulated; the large four-poster bed that we somehow shoehorned into the small bedroom, and the little things we had so much fun buying. Then, in a bittersweet moment, I tipped my cowboy hat goodbye to our small apartment and sauntered down to the local Greyhound station on my way to my new hideout – a Zen monastery in Mt. Shasta, California.

Janet: "I didn't know what to think when I found Ed's note, but I knew he was having financial problems and was trying to find a solution. Something inside of me trusted him, and I knew, sooner or later, he would contact me. So, I just kept things together while he was gone. Little did I know what was about to happen."

It was hot – a scorching 114° day in the Valley where you'd think twice before picking up a silver dollar off the sidewalk – and the bus was crowded. Busses have a distinctive smell about them; diesel mixed with . . . something. Humanity?

I never sat toward the rear of Greyhounds; strange people at times ride back there. I always tried to sit forward, directly behind the driver to keep him awake and talking in the middle of the night when his head would invariably begin to nod. These guys were good, only sleeping a few seconds before jerking their head up to drive a few miles more.

A lot of stops and a long time later, the old dog pulled around a curve on a mountain highway somewhere out of Redding – and there it was, Mt. Shasta!

It was as if its majestic snow-capped peaks were floating on a surreal, purple haze, and I felt something stir deep in the pit of my stomach; the same stirring when I left my family, and I knew the legends had it right, Mt. Shasta was surely enchanted.

The bus spit me out at the end of a beautiful afternoon. There were no cabs in sight; there was nothing in sight! It was a small town, so I had no choice but to hoof it from the bus stop up the five-mile hill to the monastery.

It didn't sound that far, so off I trudged immersed in blissful ignorance with my two bulging suitcases, a backpack, and wearing designer jeans coordinated with an expensive leather sport coat and handmade cowboy boots along, of course, with my cowboy hat. I had enough clothes to start a Goodwill store right there in the middle of Mt. Shasta.

The first mile was fun, trudging up the old asphalt road. Beginnings are always so full of energy! It was quiet, not a car or truck disturbing the setting, and the topography . . . it was strange, like nothing I had ever seen before. The volcanic activity of the past left its footprints everywhere with lava spouts and weird mounds where there shouldn't be anything at all; a bizarre carpet leading to that magnificent snowcapped mountain. The whole area was odd, in a moonscape beautiful kind of way, and forlorn with an aura of suspense and eerie silence wrapped within a million pine trees.

The cool mountain air was a heavenly relief from the broiling concrete that was Phoenix, but it was up-hill and I was carrying a lot of stuff, and the second and third mile was a little more challenging. The sun sits earlier in the mountains than it does in the flat valleys of Arizona, and for a moment, I panicked. Was this the right road? It was pretty deserted, and when night fell, it would be dark as hell. Nevertheless, I had no choice; I was way past the point of no return and could never make it back down before dark.

The sun had now gone down and the trees were slowly losing their color when suddenly, there it was! I found myself staring through the cyclone fence of a Zen monastery.

It looked quiet, deadly quiet. Only a lonely tinkling of wind chimes somewhere off in the distance disturbed the beautiful silence so characteristic of this hushed pine forest. Nobody was around except for the trees, and the ever-present pinecones – big ones.

I pulled the clapper on the old bell at the main gate and rang . . . no response. I rang again, louder . . . nothing. It was getting very dark. I followed the fence line until a glimmer of light twinkling in the trees led me to a small cabin. I walked over to the cabin and enthusiastically knocked on the door. I knew I would have to sell myself and was extremely confident that I could. I was a great salesman.

The door opened slowly, and standing on the other side was a Zen monk in a black robe with a swastika hanging on a cord around his/her neck! I couldn't distinguish a gender, and I certainly was not ready for a swastika!

"Can I help you?" she said, in a very unemotional tone. Her eyes and face were as deep and expressionless as a professional poker player, but at least I was relieved that it was a woman. She would surely be more understanding and friendly to a new, unannounced visitor, I thought, but my naivety was soon to be challenged.

"Yeah, I finally made it!" I said, smiling broadly, trying to brighten up the conversation.

"And who are you?" She replied.

"Why . . . I'm Ed Rock!" I said, while setting my bags down on the porch and dusting myself off with my cowboy hat.

She walked away unimpressed and returned with a list that she was carefully perusing.

"Nooope, I don't seem to have you on my guest list," she said, seemingly relieved, and with a look of "gotcha!" in her eyes. "When did you contact us?"

My smile melted away, along with the remaining light of evening, and that funny feeling again arose in the pit of my stomach. "Well, I haven't actually, uh, contacted anybody, but here I am, and I'm here to stay! You see . . ."

She interrupted, "You may call us in three days, if you wish. We will then discuss whether or not you may visit," and with that, she firmly closed the door.

I just stood there, stunned and staring at the door a few inches from my face. I turned around and tried to see down the mountain I had just scaled, but man, it was dark.

Okay, no problem. What the hell, it would be easier going downhill. I grabbed my bags and headed down the pitch-black hill, but this time I got lucky. After a mile or so, a pickup gave me a lift to a local motel in town.

Three days later and close to broke, I squeezed into

a phone booth and dialed the monastery as instructed – my first taste of Zen discipline. The phone rang an interminable number of times, as I silently practiced my pitch. Then somebody picked up the phone, "Shasta Abbey."

"Hello! Is this the monastery?"

"Yes, this is Shasta Abbey."

"Well, . . . hello! It's that person in town, you know, that was up there a few nights ago? Can I come back up now?"

"Just a moment please."

I held my breath. If they said no, I would really be on the run. As usual, I had no plan B, and this time no money. I heard some muted conversation in the background and finally somebody came to the phone. I recognized the voice . . . it was the monk that sent me back into town.

"May I help you?"

Wow! She sounded as cold as ever!

"It's me," I said, my usual exuberant confidence draining from my voice. "I am the guy who was there a few nights ago? I had a lot of bags. Remember? I apologize for barging in like that. I just didn't know that I had to make arrangements. Uh, is there any way that I can come up for . . . a visit? Maybe?"

"Yes, I remember you, and you may come for a short visit."

"I can?" I said in disbelief.

"Yes."

"Wow! Right on! I'm on my way! I mean, Thank you Sister, thank you!"

I hung up the phone. Yes! I made it one more day.

So, it was back up the mountain. This time, however, I unloaded most of my junk and left it in the motel. All I needed, as far as I could reckon, was a black robe and a swastika! Man, I would look so cool. I would have to take some pictures.

It was 1979 and here I was, the great Ed Rock, thirty-eight years old and hiding out in a Zen monastery. Amazing. I pictured myself having long, metaphysical discussions with Roshi Kennett, the founder of the abbey who was still alive then, but I was soon to learn the status of a newcomer at a Zen monastery, which was one of silence and obedience.

I melted into the schedule, keeping a low profile and behaving myself so I wouldn't get kicked out, and things moved along swimmingly – until I got the surprise of my life; if I intended to live long term at the monastery, I would have to ordain as a postulant and pay a hundred and twenty-five dollars a month! This was not good. I left everything with Janet in Phoenix and I was broke. Now what?

I had no choice but to dash off a letter revealing my whereabouts and invite Janet to join me, now that I knew that women could train up here, but I addressed it just 'Rock.' I didn't want the mailroom at the abbey to know her name (I had a plan). I cautioned her not to write her name or return address on the envelope with which she would reply. I didn't tell her why; I just told her to trust me.

I couldn't imagine how a shy, Catholic girl who didn't know the meaning of the word '*Zen*' except maybe when describing a sparsely furnished dorm room, would react. But she surprised me, as usual, and couldn't wait to come to Mt. Shasta even though she knew nothing about Buddhism. Her only stipulation was that I return to Phoenix and help her sell everything, except, of course, her prized Chevy Camaro.

So back down the mountain I went where I boarded my old Greydog friend and soon found myself back in sweltering Phoenix, selling or giving everything away and keeping a keen eye out for my creditors. I was slowly catching on that this 'giving away,' 'giving up' and running was becoming a way of life for us.

My grand strategy was to return to the abbey alone. I would take the bus and Janet would drive up a week later. This way, the monastery wouldn't know that we were acquainted since I wasn't sure that couples could ordain, or even stay at Shasta. I just could not stop lying about things; the truth always got in my way. But I was definitely in over my head this time; these Buddhists were very perceptive. Uncannily so.

The reality of what we were doing slowly dawned on Janet when I explained that we would have to keep our relationship under wraps for awhile (which she thought was dishonest). She would really be on her own, and she didn't know what to expect.

I made it back with no complications and was watching for her the day of her expected arrival. It was getting late and I was becoming concerned, when finally I saw her standing outside the gate with her fingers hooked through the cyclone fence, looking, with big, wide eyes, at the monks. She probably spotted the swastikas. She didn't look happy, but she either trusted or cared for me more than I realized, or perhaps both, because in she came, and was permitted to stay without going back down into town because she took my advice and called in advance.

Janet: "Eastern religions were foreign to me, I understood nothing about them, but I had always been prone to precognition. For some odd reason I had saved a newspaper article I ran across while we were in Phoenix, a piece about a monastery in Arizona and a contemplative nun, and some type of monk living with deadly snakes and diseases in a strange foreign country. I didn't know why I cut it out, or why I saved it, but as fate would have it, we would all cross paths later in Thailand, including the snakes and diseases.

Then there was my abstract watercolor in fifth grade that I named 'The Endless Journey' (Was I embarking on my endless journey now)?

The other thing that seemed to be in the realm of precognition was the high school reading assignment of the book, Siddhartha. Since I was never much a reader and tended to skim through books, it was only years later that I discovered that the book was about a very unusual man . . . Siddhartha Gautama − the Buddha!

I so hoped that this Zen monastery might offer something in the way of answers. I was depressed for many years after my mom died and I could never understand why God took her when I was very young and vulnerable, and needed her most.

The religious questioning that began at that early age continued when I found myself in grade school and warned not to associate with people unless they were Catholic. In my heart, this instruction didn't feel right or make sense and I became increasingly confused. I realized, even at that innocent age, that there were good and bad people all over the world, and I couldn't understand why their religion or race should matter.

I was initially terrified with the idea of exposing myself to a practice so foreign to my experience and giving up my psychological dependence on the Church. It was a most difficult thing, as any Catholic can imagine, even if they didn't spend twelve years in Catholic school. However, it was strangely liberating as well. Questions that had tormented me since childhood actually were being answered here at Shasta Abbey in meaningful, optimistic ways, and my mental outlook began swinging toward positive.

I found the male and female monks at the abbey to be real people, uniquely compassionate and understanding, and when I confided in them about my past, personal problems, they approached the problems in a very unusual but effective way by not specifically addressing my problems or trying to reason with me regarding them.

Instead, they gave me simple instructions on how to sit in meditation, with an open, free mind allowing the excess psychological baggage that I had been carrying around for so many years to naturally exhaust itself. My repressed, inherent wisdom that had been buried deep inside of me, covered up by all these problems, began to surface. It was a self-healing experience. I had graduated from college, but even this extensive exposure to academia could not match what I was discovering at a simple Zen monastery – meditation. It became my ultimate life saver!"

For myself, I quickly became aware that my logical, thinking mind and intelligence would not get me very far here at this monastery, about as far as a mosquito trying to bite the old Zen iron bull. Every one of my thoughts and every attempt to understand with my reasoning mind would be of no use. The only thing I could rely on now was a mysterious, deep wisdom, which supposedly was accessible through meditation.

Surprisingly, I found the experience to be quite interesting; the first vacation from thinking that my mind had ever had – it was an opportunity for the mind to relax for the first time in its life. After arriving at the abbey, overloaded with facts and idiosyncrasies and things that I knew in my head but not things that I felt in my heart, I soon discovered that meditation touched that heart directly – and it felt good.

We found that the monks at Shasta, and actually all the Buddhists we were to meet later, never instructed from an attitude of, "Believe this, this is the truth." Instead, it was a low-keyed attitude of "Consider this, and don't believe anything unless you can prove it true to yourself."

Whatever psychology was involved, it was working, and Janet was feeling better about life as she began distancing herself from her endless negative thoughts.

Janet: "One day a female Roshi explained the elementary theory of karma, or the irrefutable law of cause and effect, a law of the universe that no one can escape. This struck a deep cord in my heart, as I started seeing things from a radically different perspective, as all my past grieving and confusion began to dissolve.

For so many years, I was confused, and now for the first time in my life things began making sense. This law of karma explained why some were wealthy and others were poor, why some lived long, healthy lives while others died young, and why some were nurturing while others were murderers.

If it was true that our karma results from our own actions, in both our present and our past lives, then I could see that my mom's sufferings were possibly results of actions in previous existences and not a consequence of a God with complicated motives. This was a big relief for me!

Actually, many centuries ago, Christianity taught about pre-existing souls, or past lives, but unfortunately changed their teachings about three hundred years after Christ died. It's unfortunate because that would have made more sense to me and eased my fears. One lifetime to get it right, and if you don't you live in eternal hell, is just too condemning and just plain scary.

After an explanation of how karma and rebirth are linked, I understood that my mom died young because of some past karma, not something she did in this lifetime, because she was an extremely good person. This meant that she, or a part of her, would return to reap the good karma she made with her family this time even while going through excruciating physical and mental pain. Next time, she might even transcend material existence completely and go beyond the earth."

Chapter Three

3. The Only One You Have

Some say that Buddhism is a method to discover complete freedom within oneself, and Janet was certainly experimenting with that freedom by stepping away from the world for a moment and delving deep within herself through meditation. She was not only liberating herself from heartbreaking misunderstandings, but also discovering a new kind of release where she could seek within.

Janet: "I was being exposed to many new and astonishing possibilities, especially The Four Noble Truths that made a lot sense in explaining life to me.

"Suffering is a blessing" is a well-known Christian principle, but I could never understand how suffering could be a good thing – until now. Suffering leads to questioning, and questioning leads to observing life realistically rather than being caught up in self-pity.

The Four Noble Truths clarified all of this; especially the First Noble Truth that pointed out that life is inherently suffering. Once I understood this, I no longer felt as if I was the only one out of touch with everyone else in the world, who on the surface seemed so happy. All of us suffer in our own ways, there is no escape from it, and my acceptance of that truth changed my life. Now I could depend on myself, and my meditation, to find the answers that I had been looking for all my life.

Now that I could accept the fact that suffering was inevitable for everyone, the Second Noble Truth ex-

plained what causes the suffering. This was an epiphany for me.

The Buddha was like a physician that I went to with a problem. He first acknowledged that I had the problem, (The First Noble Truth – Suffering Exists).

Then he told me what caused it (The Second Noble Truth – Desire and Attachment are the Cause of Suffering).

He then explained further by saying that he, indeed, had a cure for this problem (The Third Noble Truth – There is a Way to End our Suffering).

Finally, he gives us a prescription to cure our problem (The Fourth Noble Truth – The Eightfold Path).

It is the last, or eighth step of this Eightfold Path that Ed and I eventually worked on the hardest. The pali translation of this eighth step describes the jhanas, loosely translated in English as meditation.

In the meantime, my favorite escape from the laundry was my 'mini-mall' (the monastery gift shop). It was such a relaxing and fun place for me with all the enticing books, cards, and knickknacks, and I escaped there whenever I could. The kitchen was also one of my favorite places. I had always wanted to learn how to prepare the wonderful vegetarian dishes, but my dreams never materialized because I was too new to take on the kitchen responsibilities and too good at doing the community laundry, something the monks noticed straightaway.

My job was to wash the monk's robes and long-term guest's clothes, except for Rev. Zenji's, (Roshi Kennett's) robes that were cared for by her personal attendants. Washing clothes every day for as many as thirty people was a challenge. The laundry room, un-

fortunately, was a dark, damp, small basement, a cave actually, with very little room and black widow and brown recluse spiders lurking in the creepy crevices.

What made the laundry job more difficult was the extremely tight monastic schedule. Every forty-five minutes, from 4:30 in the morning until 10:30 at night, a trainee must drop what she or he was doing and go on to another activity, such as breakfast, meditation sessions, work sessions, reading, classes, lunch, lectures, dinner, tea, reflection periods and on and on.

Each different activity involved a change of clothes, from work clothes, for instance, into meditation clothes. This involved going to the zendo (meditation hall), taking off our shoes, bowing at the entrance, and walking respectfully (never in a hurry) to our personal little storage area while being very quiet so we didn't disturb those who might be meditating.

Then we had to quietly grab our change of clothes, walk again respectfully to the exit of the zendo, bow reverently, put our shoes on, and go into the shower room where we changed clothes. Then, we would go back to the zendo, take off our shoes, bow, enter the zendo, put the clothes that we just changed out of back into our little storage area (quietly), bow when exiting the zendo, slip on our shoes and rush to the next activity. We had five minutes.

There was no personal time during the day, except perhaps to relieve oneself, which was to be done mindfully and quickly as well, but the schedule didn't bother Ed at all. He was the type to drop things quickly and start something new just as fast. I was another story. I was a plodder, slow to get going and hesitant to stop, and although the schedule for me was stress-

ful, it effectively began to teach me in small ways how to give up my attachments. I formed attachments easily. Anything that I found pleasurable I would grasp at and hang on to for dear life. Of course, when that pleasurable thing changed, disappeared or whatever, I would suffer.

The monastery had only two washing machines, with only one usually working, and no dryer, so timing things between activities was a challenge. Drying clothes during the winter months was especially difficult requiring me to hang them in the shower room all the way on the other side of the grounds where there was a little heat. On sunny days I had the luxury of hanging clothes outside on a clothesline, which was a great treat, not only because of the two monastery dogs, 'Imadog' and 'Uradog' that were tied close by (I really liked animals), but because I could get out of my little prison of a laundry room for awhile.

Three months at the monastery and many baskets of clothes later, I made a big decision; I parked my cherished Camaro in town at a local gas station with a for sale sign in the window. It was my first new one and I was afraid that I would miss it because it was one of my big attachments. As it turned out, I became so involved preparing for my ordination that I didn't even have time to grieve when it quickly sold.

In order to ordain as postulants, we had to prepare in several different ways. For one, we had to make our own robes, two of them. I had never made my own clothes growing up but was accustomed to hand sewing, whereas for Ed, the prospect of sewing was appalling. He would rather dig graves! He accepted it as a challenge, however, and rationalized that if the other male monks somehow got through it, he would

30

too!"

My first robe literally took weeks to complete as I spent all of my elective activity periods in the sewing room swearing under my breath, "What the hell is a blind stitch?" But the second robe, ahh . . . it only took me three hours.

Janet: "When the time came to have our heads shaved, (shaving the head was symbolic of letting go of worldly attachments), I was not ecstatic. Amazingly, however, like many things I experienced at the abbey, it wasn't as bad as I feared when all my blonde tresses disappeared.

Everything at the monastery was having a positive effect and changing my life in many ways, so positive in fact that cutting off my hair became not only incidental but had an upside as well; I no longer had to agonize over dirty hair! We could only take a shower every three days and we had to take 'seaman's showers' where we would wet ourselves down, shut off the water, soap up, and then rinse off quickly using only a gallon or so of water. How I missed those hot, luxurious twenty-minute showers in Phoenix."

There was an interesting progression at Shasta. Monks could only advance to Roshi status after two things occurred – first, they were required to experience a first 'kensho,' or significant understanding leading to enlightenment. This understanding had to be certified by Roshi Kennett. Secondly, they had to be in robes for at least five years.

These rules were in place to make sure that a monk taught from insight – an expanded place in his or her heart, and not from mere book learning. It also was to insure that the monk had control of his or her desires to the extent that they could function without being influenced by the inherent greed, hatred, and delusion of the world.

A new Roshi would teach only simple meditation instructions until they acquired the additional compassion and wisdom to conduct classes that were more involved. Therefore, becoming a teacher at Shasta required authentic spiritual development and not so much IQ.

Janet: "The Roshis provided guidance and classes at the abbey, teaching gently, little by little, and allowing time for me to integrate my meditation into my life. Too many instructions at this point would have confused me. The compassionate, truthful, and wise council of these Roshis relaxed my mind and simplified my life in many ways, and opened new perspectives in my life.

A good example was my introduction to the Buddha's life and his Four Noble Truths. These made it clear to me why things happen in the manner that they do; why we are born, why we die, how we should live our lives and how we should practice if we truly want to become enlightened beings.

In addition, I was beginning to understand why Ed left his family because the Buddha faced a similar situation. The Buddha walked away from his palace, his wife, and newborn son because he could not understand why we are born, why we die, and how it is all connected. He had to find the deathless. So I was not only experiencing new perspectives resulting from meditation practice, but I was getting sorely needed explanations about life."

As for myself, I merely did what they told me to do just so I wouldn't be asked to leave. Where would I go? The world I was familiar with was admittedly slowly falling apart, yet the spiritual life was nowhere to be found. It was the jumping off place for all seekers.

I was assigned to the goat department. My job was to graze the baby goats on the mountainside every day among the manzaneta patches (except on the days when it snowed up to three feet at a time). I also helped a young monk milk the mature goats and assisted in birthing, feeding, and pen repairs. The goat milk and cheese supplied much-needed protein to supplement our semi-vegetarian diet, and the goats themselves provided a lot of fun.

They were characters, from the dominant females who would stand like statues on the highest thing they could find, to the bashful ones who would hide under the mangers all day. Especially comical were the frisky males who would regularly crash through stout, barbed wire fences hoping for a shot at the female population.

My young colleague and I got along well because neither of us liked to talk much, usually not more than a sentence or two. One morning, after it had been raining hard for three straight days, as it often does around Mt. Shasta, we were filling sinks with cold water to cool down fresh buckets of warm goat milk, and I as looked out at the dreary landscape from a smeared window of the goat building, I muttered under my breath "Another crummy day." My monk friend turned the water off for a moment, glanced out the window at the rain-drenched landscape, and mused, "But it's the only one I have."

That was so cool, so authentic. Those were the kinds of words that had a tendency to stick in my mind, and I have since tried to spend each day as if it were the only one I had.

One day my monk friend didn't show up, which was unusual, and I wondered if he was ill. The following day, however, he was back at work but he wasn't the same monk. Something had undeniably happened to him. This change in personality was my first positive proof that something was definitely going on up here. I asked around and found out that he had experienced a first 'kensho,' the initial meditation flash or experience where the bottom of 'reality' drops out, qualifying a monk to become a Roshi providing that he or she spends the required five years at the monastery.

For three days, my monk friend stumbled around in wonderment looking at nature and saying things such as, "Wow," or "I can't believe it." He didn't talk to me directly, but I could tell that he had definitely gone through a life-altering experience and he was never the same afterward as if some old soul had taken over his body.

For the first six months, the monastic schedule for Janet and I was brutal. If I had someone to write to, which I didn't, I wouldn't have had time to scratch out a postcard. Even if I would have found time to write, I decided to avoid dividing my kid's allegiances between their mom and me, or later between their new dad and me, who was soon to arrive on the scene. He was one of my best friends in high school and lived on a little farm right down the road when we were kids. I couldn't count the times he and I slept in the hay barn or tobogganed together in the pasture. He was the original nice guy. No, I had done enough damage already. I decided not to bother them further.

Although I had no personal time to spare, I was permitted to engage in elective activities so I used my time making 'mangis' in the shop. The ancient Buddhist 'manji' represented infinity and the seal of the Buddha's heart, but it was pirated by Hitler's regime and renamed a 'swastika' after reversing the points from left to right. I was glad to get that cleared up!

You could find me in the shop making manjis from all kinds of materials – copper, wood, plastic, stainless steel, or almost any material I could get my hands on – and I became so good at it that I had waiting lists of orders from both the monks and the gift shop.

What almost did me in however, were the meditation periods in the zendo, only because I was so stubborn and vain.

Janet: "Ed's legs were very muscular from playing football and had zero flexibility. Me? I had no problems whatsoever! I was a little quiet butterfly; he was a bull in a China shop!

For me, however, the mental aspects of meditation were a challenge. The first adjustment was sitting a foot from a wall and staring at it with half-closed eyes. This was entirely new to me. Then, it took awhile to catch on to watching each individual thought as a separate entity rather than a continuing storyline in my head.

I could not figure out how this process was going to help, as nothing was being explained – I was just told to sit there watching my thoughts.

I thought to myself, "Thinking was no different from what I had done all my life, and what was so special about doing it here?" I failed to recognize, however, that my entire life was endlessly involved and caught up in my thoughts, rather than simply observing them. This passive observation that I was now working with made all the difference. This break in the endless thoughts created a space where the mind mysteriously expanded.

I was finally able to distance the mind from the inevitable depression resulting from thoughts spiraling downwards when I discovered that I was not my thoughts. They were just momentary, random pulses of consciousness that arose and disappeared in my mind. They were not me.

I discovered this when I was told to imagine myself perched on top of a freeway overpass watching the cars and trucks go by underneath, being careful not to climb into any of them and go for a ride. The cars and trucks of course represented my thoughts, which I would look at as if they belonged to somebody else, and hopefully weakening my personal relationship with them. I was supposed to watch each thought until it disappeared on its own, being cautious not to lose my attention. Surprisingly, I quickly discovered that the mere awareness of thoughts usually weakened their presence, and that whatever was watching the thoughts was extremely intelligent!"

When I first arrived, I thought it would only take a few months to become enlightened; after all, I had the smarts, and had always accomplished whatever I wanted in life quickly and easily with no problems whatsoever. But surprise! Instead of becoming enlightened, I almost killed my knees! Meditation, to this day, has never turned out to be what I expected – physically, mentally, or spiritually.

The first time was the worst; a monk had instructed me that afternoon on how to sit on the meditation cushion with my legs crossed. It was simple, really. This wasn't exactly rocket science. That evening, I arrived at the zendo and was shown where to sit, which was directly in front of a Roshi. He was two feet behind me staring at my head. No problem. So I sat down and assumed the perfect position. I would show Roshi how to meditate!

I crossed my legs and even put one foot on top of my opposite thigh, which is how many of the monks sat. I looked good. I sat up really straight. I was a Buddha statue. The bell rang and there was nothing but silence. Nobody in the whole zendo moved as much as an eyelid – and I did look good. In about five minutes, however, the pain began.

Nevertheless, I was determined not to move. At about ten minutes into the forty-minute period, I began to sweat a little, but still didn't move. I couldn't see my watch without looking down, and since I would have rather died than move and show weakness to my Roshi friend sitting behind and staring at the back of my head, I gutted it out. It must be near the end of the period, I thought frantically, and that any moment the bell would ring. But it didn't, and the pain was like hot lightning shooting up my back and down my legs. It was surreal. It took over my whole being. Why wasn't the damn bell ringing? Did someone forget? Now I was getting angry, but still I didn't move.

After what seemed like two hours, I was tempted

to move my legs ever so slowly so that the unblinking eyes behind me wouldn't notice, but my legs were locked in place and dead like two discarded logs. I was trapped. How long could legs remain numb before they had to be cut off, I wondered. Amputated legs, however, could not match my vanity and I continued not to move – and then the bell rang.

Still, I couldn't move. I had to use my hands to straighten out my numb legs and prop them up until the feeling came back. I was afraid to look behind me and see what the Roshi thought about all of this, but when I did, he just smiled and nodded. I guess I did good.

I got smart fast as far as my meditation posture was concerned. I learned how to sit just on the tip of the pillow so my legs wouldn't fall asleep, and how to position my legs so that the pain was bearable. However, the meditation sessions continued to remain excruciatingly painful with my muscular, inflexible legs twisted up like pretzels and motionless for forty minutes at a time, but nothing compared to that first experience.

The pain would always begin slowly, steadily increasing in intensity until I thought I could no longer stand it. Only then, would it break and soon start building again. Somehow, however, I got through it all thanks to pure grit and ingenuity. I would imagine the pain as a big pizza where I removed one slice of the pain at a time and ate it. When that didn't work, I would try to determine if the pain was in my head or in my knees, or perhaps in my nerves between my head and my knees, and then concentrate on the area where I thought it was. We were permitted to move, of course, and were encouraged to do so if the position became painful, but I was too vain to move and thus became well acquainted with not only the cycles of pain, but with my arrogance as well.

Luckily for me, it was some time before the monastery had a '*sessin*', an intensive week of fourteen, one-hour periods of sitting and walking meditation each day. That was a challenge!

Eventually I became accustomed with the position and the pain stopped, and only then did I discover what meditation was really all about.

In the beginning, I physically feared meditation, but later I feared it psychologically, worried this inner reflection would weaken the authority of my strong-willed mind. This is the reason that I hesitated to begin this practice in the first place back in Phoenix; I didn't want to risk trading control of my faculties for an outside chance that I might someday come face-to-face with whatever enlightenment is. I wanted a contract, a sure clad agreement before experimenting with my mind.

Out in the world, I would never have taken even a few minutes out of my frantic routine to meditate. I was too busy racing around and around on my never ending carousel of illusions, and spending every waking moment storing up the money and experiences that I foolishly could only borrow for the short time that I would be on this earth. As a result, I only pretended to meditate at first.

I went through the motions of stillness, but I still craved excitement; I was a thrill seeker. If I didn't keep myself busy with one activity after another, an empty feeling crept in and I would become despondent and bored. I was extremely clever at escaping this boredom; however, I could easily create situations to relieve the boredom and emptiness and satisfy my desires. Down deep, however, I had a nagging, inexpressible feeling that I was only playing with a world that, in the end, could not sustain me. Maybe everything was just a passing parade that would eventually march out of sight.

I feared emptiness because it might reveal a truth that would slap me rather than hug me, and such a truth remained far too dangerous for my small, worldly mind to face. In no way could I relate to a reality that was so far removed from existence, as I knew it; I would just have to experience it, right here at Shasta, so I began to experiment.

What if my mind really could remain empty but at the same time remain incredibly aware? Could I shut down my core need of excitement instead escaping into it? Could I remain within the emptiness? What would that be like? Could I ever find peace within a mind like mine that was always in turmoil and wanted only to control things? How could I go beyond this ongoing confusion and find that 'something?'

It was obvious that the first step would involve an observation of my mind until I understood everything about it. How else would its mystique vanish? I had to face the fact that the only things ever to hold my interest were things that remained a mystery to me. Therefore, in order to get beyond my mind, I would have to solve the mind's mystery as well, so I took the Zen advice to – study my mind until I understood my mind, and once I understood my mind, I could forget my mind, and once I could forget my mind, I could become enlightened.

The hours I initially spent in meditation were interminable with pain taking up all my attention, but then as my legs adapted and the pain eased, I was able to watch my mind, beginning with my thoughts.

The thoughts finally calmed down when I watched my thoughts, as we were instructed to do by the monks, by watching our thoughts as if we were standing on a bridge watching the traffic pass below.

Once the thoughts calmed down and were absent for rather long periods of time, I noticed the only other thing that was going on – my solar plexus just above my belly button was rising and falling with my breathing. After a short while, even that sensation faded into the background with nothing remaining except a delicious, complete awareness of nothingness. Once I decided to surrender and follow the monks' instructions, meditation became easy, and it wasn't long before my understanding of rebirth became a personal experience rather than a mere intellectual assumption!

Since we meditated facing a plywood paneled wall with our eyes half open and half closed, my usual pastime was finding all kinds of designs in the paneling to occupy myself. One particular day, as I was perusing the plywood, I suddenly found myself in a desert! I wasn't dreaming that I was in a desert; I was actually in a desert! The yellow-white sand was blinding and I could feel a relentless sun that revealed before me broad white steps leading to . . . nothing. It was as if I was a camera filming myself standing half way up the steps. Beside me on the steps was another man wearing an orange robe whose head was shaved. I was dressed in a white robe with my head shaved as well, which was all very puzzling to me. The only robes I had ever seen were Catholic robes and the black robes of the monks here at Shasta. Only after I went to Thailand three years later did I see the orange robes of the monks and the white robes of the layman. The man in the orange robe standing on the steps then put his hand on my shoulder and said, "Go to your father."

Go to my father? What did that mean? The orange robed man no sooner uttered those four words than the scene abruptly changed. Now I found myself on a narrow city street lined with shops. The cars parked on the street indicated the early 1940s, about the era I was born. In this scene, my 'camera' was now observing everything from ground level as if looking up from a curb. I strangely knew that I was looking at myself, which, in this case, was a young woman. She was walking arm in arm with another young woman, both sporting hair styles of the forties and dressed in tailored gray suits that were fashionable in that era. The scene was in black and white, sharply contrasting the brilliant desert setting of the previous scene. Then in a flash, I was back staring at the plywood in the zendo.

Whoa! What the hell just happened? It wasn't as if I fell asleep and had a dream. This was not a dream; it was too sharp in all its details and my dreams never involved historical periods, and further, my head remained upright and still. It wasn't a vision of some kind because I somehow knew that I was actually there. I was at a loss for words, but it was real, and even though I usually kept things to myself, I couldn't wait for the meditation period to end so that I could talk to a Roshi about it. I was certain that the Roshi's response would be, "It's only 'makyo,' (visions and voices that arise in meditation that one should ignore)," but regardless, I was anxious to inquire.

I ran after a Roshi who had just left the zendo and was walking briskly toward the kitchen. When I caught up to her and described my experience, she looked at me quizzically and replied matter-of-factly, "You experienced a glimpse of two past lives." Then she added, "Hmm, it's unusual, especially for a new meditator, but don't become overly excited about the experience. Just continue with your meditation as if nothing had happened. Past life experiences are commonplace occurrences around here."

Wow! Pretend it didn't happen? Fat chance. This just proved to me beyond any doubt that more was going on in this universe than I could ever wrap my puny intellect around. It was amazing, authentic and I couldn't get it out of my mind.

I wasn't the type to be easily fooled or influenced; I was engaged in the business world far too long for any kind of "New Age" nonsense and was more inclined toward critical and scientific observation. Let's face it; I was downright cynical! But this blew my mind. It just wasn't within the parameters of anything that I had ever experienced before or even imagined.

I could see now that only an undisturbed mind, a mind that was kept calm and silent for long periods of time, could plumb the depths of that mystical world within. I also could see how stress and turmoil prohibits this from happening in modern-day lives. Before coming to Shasta, I was so crude that I would have been fortunate for even an occasional peek inside, if that, but now my inner world was finally revealing itself.

Christians never talked about past life experiences when I was growing up, even though Christians reportedly believed in preexisting souls at least until sometime after Christ died when during some big meeting they decided not to.

Actually, Catholics St. John of the Cross and St. Teresa of Avila were meditators, something I would never have known about if their books were not required reading at the abbey. They were Christian contemplatives and in many ways close to Buddhists. In his masterpiece, 'The Ascent of Mount Carmel,' St. John said, "And the fourth degree of evil that comes from joy of worldly things is: And he departed from God, his salvation. This man has made money and things of the world his God, and David said, 'Be thou not afraid when a man shall be made rich, for when he dieth, he shall carry nothing away, neither riches, nor joy, nor glory."

Janet: "I never knew that there was a deeper side of Christianity, and most all religions. In Christianity, it is called Christian Mysticism, and until Shasta Abbey, I wasn't aware of it. Nobody in the Catholic Church ever mentioned it. I also didn't realize that St. Teresa of Avila, a cloistered nun, and St. John of the Cross practiced and taught contemplative prayer which is similar to beginning meditation. I wish the Catholic Church had tuned into this when I was growing up. It would have answered many of my questions because meditation seems to touch the heart in ways that mere words fail. The Church does seem to be coming around, but I fear that it's going to take a long time to change entrenched beliefs."

Like an illness slowly eating away at my heart until only a shell is left, I, too, made money and things my god, and the consequences would certainly have left me shipwrecked in a self-made hell where escape was no longer possible. Ironically, however, while looking for a place to hide from my bill collectors, I accidentally came across this life raft of an abbey. How could I expect my meditation to deepen, however, without my intentions changing? What results could I expect if I forced my mind to be still during meditation but then behaved recklessly later, even if only in my mind? That was where I must begin, by honestly stopping and looking at myself if I truly wanted to change; and I did want to.

For a long time my ego convinced me that I was perfect, but nobody is − they just don't look closely enough. The problem was, if I stopped lying to myself, what choice would I have but to become responsible, and that wouldn't be easy after all these years of recklessness. How did I end up like this, leaving my family and hiding out in Zen Monastery?

Chapter Four

4. The Vow

One morning, after an unusually calm period of meditation, I was walking in the woods behind the meditation hall when I became mesmerized with the rising sun reflecting off dew-covered pine needles. I softly touched their exquisite aliveness, and as I did, emotions unexpectedly overwhelmed me for no apparent reason. I began to cry, sob really, with my whole body shaking. I wasn't sad, I wasn't happy; I was just mysteriously overwhelmed with rapture.

I heard somebody walking behind me and felt a hand on my shoulder. It was one of the senior monks. I was embarrassed for crying because there was no reason in my mind to be emotional, so my mind quickly thought up an excuse for the tears, as I blurted out, "Someday, I will have to leave all of this beauty behind."

He kindly looked into my eyes for a moment and then replied, "Yes, you will, Edward. And it will be okay." I think he knew that I was just making an excuse to hide an overwhelming bliss that came out of left field. Why did my mind have to make an excuse? Maybe the mind was conditioned to believe that '*real*' men didn't cry, at least that was what the world had taught me.

So now I was stuck. It was too late to return to that world I was familiar with, and yet I could not see my way forward either. I was trapped with no way out. What choice did I now have but to continue my struggles, both here at this monastery and in my search for enlightenment?

Finding this truth had unexpectedly become a life's mission, a passion. I was convinced that it unlocked the hidden secret of contentment regardless of external events, and I had a feeling that I was closing in on it. What else could I do now but forge ahead? Nothing in this fleeting world would ever interest me again, except for this, thus far, inaccessible truth that I was certain I would find. I was becoming confident that I would somehow make my way back to a place in my heart that had been vacant far too long.

Meditation spawned hints of truth that were swimming past my mind and lodging in my heart. This created permanent shifts in the depths of my being, channeling my life into unexplored waters with strong, overwhelming feelings that were coming from places with which I was unfamiliar. Everything was changing. I became sensitive to each and every action, and painfully aware whenever I hurt people or caused them to feel uncomfortable even in small ways. I was finding that I just couldn't do that anymore regardless of the cost to myself.

Janet: "Conversation was not encouraged at the abbey, actually it was more or less forbidden. We spent the entire day in silent contemplation or meditation, talking only when necessary during work periods or during group discussions. Ed loved it, but then of course, he was always the quiet type. Even as a kid, his mother would say that he was a "man of few words."

My mind was becoming exceptionally calm; precisely how calm I didn't appreciate until I unmindfully ran a large sliver of wood in my arm while working on the goat pens. This involved a trip into Mt. Shasta for a tetanus shot, my first trip out of the mountains since I arrived, and the experience was astounding. It was surprising how the traffic, the people, everything seemed to be moving in fast motion, yet indicative of how calm the mind had become without my realizing it.

I couldn't help notice the sadness of the faces in the cars we passed, yet each would probably insist that he or she was very happy. It is such a big step to admit that one suffers. Such a basic, simple thing is rarely expressed, perhaps because we cover it up so well.

Except for Roshi Kennett and a few of her assistant monks, the rest of the community of about thirty, plus guests, all slept in the zendo on the same carpeted, raised platform, about thirty inches high, that we meditated on. Each individual bed on the platform was about three feet wide separated by a one-inch strip of wood and extending six feet from the exterior walls. Built into the wall were small cabinets, one for each three-foot section that served as the occupant's one and only storage area for personal belongings such as clothes, shoes, and sleeping bags.

Men and women were considered equal in all ways at Shasta, but at night, we slept in separate areas divided by portable screens. The little, laughable electric heaters scattered about the mammoth hall didn't help at all during the winter months with temperatures dipping regularly into the low forties inside the sleeping area. Thank goodness for sleeping bags, and woe to the trainee who had to pee in the middle of the night.

Not only was it freezing, but the creaky floors would awaken everybody in the immediate area who would sleepily look around to see who the culprit was that had to pee as the pee-er attempted to inconspicuously make it to the bathroom outside the freezing hall. As a result, very little tea was consumed after six p.m.

Meals were eaten in silence at long tables where plates of food were handed down, one-way, from the front of the table to the back with each person taking their share and passing it on. The plates went by only once, so we had to estimate how many people were at the table and accordingly take only an amount that would insure that everybody else down the line would receive an equal share. There were no seconds.

My first meal at the abbey was such a disaster and teaching that I will never forgot it.

I didn't know how things worked, that first time, and I was really hungry, so to me this was just a football training table where I assumed a big guy like me could take as much food as he needed.

With this rationale, I took about half the food on each plate that came by, leaving little for those further down the line. How embarrassing when about half way through the meal, I discovered how things worked, noticing only a few spoonsful of food on each of the monks' plates at the end of the table.

A fourth grade Catholic school experience suddenly flashed through my mind where I made a mistake as well, unwittingly putting my lunch box on the wrong shelf and being hit by a nun, but this time instead of being punished or reprimanded, nobody seemed to notice.

Without the distraction of criticism, I was able to

see my greed clearer than I had ever seen it before, and I felt terrible. I wanted to apologize, but since the meals were eaten in silence (everything was in silence), I could only agonize about my gluttony while watching everybody down the line quietly eating what little they had. This time I had no Catholic Sister to blame; I could only blame myself, and it had an impact.

The food itself was unbelievably delicious and healthy as well. Who would have thought that vegetarian cooking could be tastier than 'regular' food? Perhaps everything seemed better at Shasta in that thin mountain air, or maybe it was the meditation. Was it the balance I was developing between my body and mind? The regular schedule, no worldly stress and associating with kind, non-judgmental people were quite a change from where I was coming from.

Janet: "I was thriving too. Sugar and sweets, and especially cookies aggravated my moodiness and lack of energy, and since these were not to be found in abundance at the abbey, I was feeling great. Breakfast would include granola, oatmeal, eggs, French toast, nuts, pancakes, fruit, and little surprises of all kinds. Lunch would be even better with vegetarian dishes that were no less works of art and love with vegetarian lasagna, goat cheeses and milk, homemade bread, tofu, rice of every description, other soy products, vegetables, and delicious sauces. Dinner was a 'medicine meal' and very light, usually just soup and perhaps some bread with a tofu or miso spread. I didn't realize that healthy, vegetarian food could taste so good.

The monk in charge of the kitchen had been the

chief cook at the abbey for many years and was superb at it, very focused. He would always do his best to weigh the wellbeing of his monks against his meager budget, and would agonize over adding one extra egg to a large recipe while scouring local markets for deals on fruits and vegetables."

Of the many things Janet and I learned at Shasta, one of the most penetrating concerned life and how life involves going beyond limitations that we usually only place on ourselves. We were also discovering the uniqueness of meditation; an experience far removed from any particular religion or belief, but at the same time easily accommodating them all.

Although meditation helped us reach beyond our old conclusions that lurked in our brains, words can't come close to describing something so profound, something that we could only feel in our hearts.

'Practicing' meditation at the abbey was not the same as 'meditating.' Meditation had a mind of its own, and we were never sure, when it was going to show up.

Things were going well, extremely well. My ego had always thought that I was out of the ordinary, that nothing could ever happen to me because I was somehow protected. I was special, and other people, who were not exceptional like me, had accidents and misfortune.

Then, out of left field, as if to teach my ego a lesson, the illness hit.

Initially when I first arrived at Shasta, I experienced some chronic diarrhea for a few weeks, but one session of acupressure with a Roshi cured that. This, however, was more serious; this felt like complete exhaustion. A Roshi diagnosed my problem as 'Zen sickness,' a strange malady that occurs when internal or spiritual passages, akin to acupuncture meridians, become blocked and confused for various reasons. One reason could be that a meditator with a coarse mind (maybe somebody running from his creditors?) suddenly begins meditating for long, intense periods without first cultivating gentleness, compassion and loving-kindness!

The illness worsened, notwithstanding visits by a local doctor. Zen sickness is apparently not treatable by traditional Western medicine and is therefore difficult to diagnose or treat. Acupressure treatments by the Roshis didn't help either, and I was eventually confined to the dark, dreary 'sick' cabin, that had no windows and a single candle.

As I laid there, I found myself thinking about all the people who selflessly helped me throughout my life, taking me under their wings as if I were the most important person in the world. In this decisive moment, lying in the dark, sick as a dog, and clearly seeing my own unrelenting self-centeredness, all I could envision were the graves I helped dig at the abbey's cemetery. I had a stone-cold feeling that I wasn't going to make it this time and I was certain that the cemetery was my next stop.

Fear and death were closing in; I could tangibly feel them. The mounting panic had not yielded to the heavenly peace that arrives just before the end, a serenity experienced once before when I was eighteen and almost drowned in Lake Erie. Actually, neither fear nor death would have concerned me had I nothing left to lose, but I had plans. My life still lacked . . . something. And because of that something, I was not ready to die – not quite yet, because here I was, desperately clinging to life with all my strength, hoping beyond hope that something would rescue me. When the illness worsened, however, I handled it as I had handled everything in the past – by running.

Janet: "We bussed down from Mt. Shasta to the Bay Area and rented a small apartment in Lafayette. I went to work at a stationery store while Ed took a job at a Radio Shack, knowing that he couldn't stay long before some creditor would track him down through his employment records.

We both walked to work, since driving was too aggressive to our minds that had become extremely sensitive, even if we had a car. We had no choice but to desensitize our minds in some fashion, a desensitizing process that had the unfortunate result of impeding any further insights from arising for the time being."

I needed somewhere to chill out. The Zen sickness wasn't improving and I was getting bone-tired of looking over my shoulder for bill collectors. I knew that I had to change things up, so one afternoon I again left Janet a note and headed for Tennessee with a bus ticket and a few bucks in my pocket. I only hoped that they would take me in at 'The Farm,' the famous commune headed up by the original San Francisco hippie-refugee, Stephen Gaskin. It was advertised as a very spiritual place. As I boarded the old grey dog, I noticed that the smell hadn't changed.

Janet: "I was getting accustomed to Ed going off by himself to get some space, so I gathered everything up and went to live at a branch of Shasta Abbey in

Oakland to await his return.

The Oakland Priory was just a big house in a questionable low rent area with about eight residents, but safe enough for me to ride the train back and forth to my job at the stationary store in Lafayette. I always loved to go into stationary stores, like Hallmark, and look around, and now I worked in one!

Like a lost puppy, I knew Ed would be back soon, probably less than a year, and that he would try to contact me through the abbey. In the meantime, I could get some funds together. I knew he would come back broke, as usual!"

I made it to Summertown, Tennessee and hitched a ride from the bus station to walking distance of The Farm. I was feeling on top of the world and wildly anticipating the great new experiences ahead. This was always my reaction when leaving a monastery, taking all the accumulated good karma and blowing it as soon as possible.

I walked a couple of miles down a dirt road until I came across a rundown two-story garage type building in the middle of nowhere. I was hoping that this wasn't 'The Farm' but my hopes were soon dashed. A longhaired hippie was guarding the gate.

While mentally kicking myself for not doing my homework before literally spending my life's savings on a cross-country bus ticket, the gatekeeper invited me in with a stern warning not to go beyond the gatehouse. So there I stayed for the better part of a week sleeping in a loft with people from all over the world, and being interviewed and eyeballed by a constant stream of hippies asking unusual questions.

The Farm, I was to discover, was chockfull of

women and kids at a ratio of about thirteen hundred women and kids to two hundred men, so newcomers were justifiably screened vigilantly. I must have answered all the questions more or less correctly because one morning I was escorted from the gatehouse to the main compound about half a mile away. From there, a hippie took me to a small three-bedroom house with an attic loft that would be my new home that I would share with six men, ten women, and eleven kids. The Farm routinely put word out to young women all over the country that if they have a kid and no 'old man' to take care of them, they were welcome to live on The Farm.

The soy dairy, the bakery, and the kitchen fed the entire community and were the centers of activity, so the dairy was my first assignment. We would soak hundreds of pounds of soybeans overnight in huge tubs and process them the next day into tofu, tempeh, miso, soymilk, and soy ice cream as moms lined up with their five-gallon buckets at the windows. After a short career at the dairy, I helped The Farming crew hand plant fifteen acres of tomato plants, before landing a job on the masonry crew where we trucked sixty miles north to the Nashville area every day to build solar houses.

The Farm was extremely active with many cottage industries – home building, tie dyed T-shirts, professional bands that toured the country, nuke busters (small, hand-held devices to detect radiation from clandestine government trucks illegally transporting nuclear materials), and other ingenious entrepreneurial endeavors such as a vegetarian restaurant in Nashville. These all helped support the commune that, per person, spent about fifty cents a day to feed everyone.

We ate lots of soybeans, baked our own bread, grew our own vegetables and hoped that some of the folks' parents would kick in some money, or at least some peanut butter and Hershey bars.

Mysteriously, the Zen sickness disappeared completely. I didn't know at the time, how the spiritual world worked, and that this was only a brief respite from burning up my past karma – karma that I would eventually have to face again – big time!

I had the privilege of becoming acquainted with many kind folks who were each spiritual in their own special way, from my skinny, scarred friend who lost his scalp after tangling his long hair in a potato-picking machine, to friends I had scattered here and there all over the commune. We had doctors and attorneys, a few dentists, and lots of love.

Everybody took a vow of poverty when entering the commune, giving up all of their worldly possessions (easy for me to do), so that everybody was in the same boat, and all seemingly in the same house – mine! The married folks and the kids slept in the three bedrooms downstairs while the single people slept in a sea of sleeping bags in the loft.

My routine was to get up at four thirty a.m., collect my bagged lunch at the food area (three bean salad and tofu), and then squeeze into a pickup truck with as many hippies that would fit before we headed for Nashville. We'd all toke up a couple of times on the way, insuring mass confusion upon our arrival at the job sight as we all ran around trying to remember what the hell we were supposed to do, or even where we were! Then somebody would yell, "Let's mix cement" and we'd all head for the cement mixer due to Mary Wonder's incredible suggestiveness. Once we got down to business, however, with supervisors setting out lines and excavators doing their thing, we actually built better solar homes than the State of Tennessee, and way less expensive!

Shortly after the 'four o'clock vibes' where everyone would become negative for half an hour, we would head back to The Farm where we would arrive toward evening covered in cement dust, dirty as crime, and facing cold showers. The only hot water in the house relied on our ingenious hippie solar water heater that consisted of a long black hose spread out on the roof soaking up the sun's rays. The women and kids always had first shot at the little bit of hot water that the hose produced, and that was okay with me.

The local cops tolerated our driving back and forth to Nashville for unknown, magical reasons; and late one night, after working a few days at The Farm's vegetarian restaurant, we tested the cops once again.

Twelve of us, all very high and packed like sardines in a dilapidated van, were trying to make it back to The Farm, but as usual, we were running on empty. We stopped for gas but faced a dilemma. Actually, the dilemma was easing in directly behind us with its high beams on two feet away from the rusted rear bumper of our old van.

Our driver stumbled out of the van trying to look as composed as a high hippie can, and, of course, couldn't find the gas tank. The two officers slid out of their patrol car and approached cautiously with their hands on their weapons, pointing out the gas tank to the driver and saying that everything was cool, and that they were just going to ask a few questions.

Well, we all thought it was over for this bunch of hippies as our driver dove back into the van rummaging through the glove box looking for non-existent papers and mumbling that we would all have to get out. We knew we were busted!

Trying desperately not to break up laughing, we obediently fell out of the van as casually as we could knowing that if one of us started giggling, it would all be over. So, biting our tongues and attempting to look very square (hard to do), we all just stood there lined up against the gas pumps – a motley crew if there ever was one with discarded clothes and mismatched socks.

I overheard the woman officer mentioning to our driver, that the plates were expired, which was a chronic problem with our junk vehicles, and asking if we were from The Farm. He confessed that we were, and then asked if she had heard about our free ambulance service in New York; or about our work in Guatemala where we were setting up soy dairies to help the poor folks get a little protein down there, and I had a hunch that maybe, just maybe, we were saved once again!

A few minutes later, the male officer wrote out a ticket for expired plates and said that we had better be careful driving down to Summertown, after which they got in their cruiser and left!

We all looked at each other in amazement, and never did find out whether they were really cool cops, or maybe just going off-duty soon and didn't want to process a humongous drug bust! Either way, we were all spared some complications in our lives – for real, man!

The evenings on The Farm were mystical, filled with soft sounds of strumming guitars, laughing kids, and the unmistakable subtle wafting of pot. Marijuana was considered a religious sacrament, no different from peyote that sustained American Indians for 10,000 years, and since pot was therefore considered sacred, only certain authorized elder hippies had access to the supply that was divvied out to the community a few times a day.

To catch my early ride to Nashville, I was usually up before anybody else, and unfortunately the first one in the kitchen. This was unfortunate because I had to face the hordes of roaches by myself. The whole place would be crawling with roaches; big ones, baby ones and all kinds, all over the place. They were everywhere, under the stools and chairs, in the pans and stove, and in every crevice. It would look as if the whole top of the kitchen counter was moving.

Being pacifists and all, we of course couldn't kill them, but the moms were concerned about their kids' health and continued to grumble, as good moms do.

One evening we resignedly gathered around for our fifth cockroach meeting. We had tried everything imaginable of a peaceful nature; psychic triangles in every corner, sound vibrations, visualizing them gone, etc., but nothing seemed to work. It was time for drastic action.

After passing around a couple of joints − it was against the rules to smoke marijuana alone, which was considered selfish and not at all spiritual, we decided that we had no choice but to begin destroying the roaches. We would apportion the dastardly deed of killing a household total of one hundred a day, each of us with a quota, and we appointed a mom to keep track. We were required to turn in the dead little bodies.

That night we all went to bed dreading the thought

that tomorrow we would all become cold-blooded killers. Cockroaches were incredibly clever, intelligent beings when observed, with their advance scouts and the methods in which they communicated with each other, and with their legions in our kitchen, it was almost impossible not to observe them!

Early the next morning, I crept into the kitchen with my fly swatter at the ready, reluctantly preparing to kill my 3.7 roaches for the day, but guess what; there were no roaches! I quickly roused everybody and in a few minutes, the entire household was all standing around in the kitchen staring in disbelief. We came up with a few stray roaches, but no more than you would normally find in any house out in the country.

No roaches were killed that day!

That evening, with furrowed brows, we passed a joint around again, our sixth roach meeting. We decided that the roaches must be psychic and could obviously read minds because they knew our intentions ahead of time, and that killing such special beings would, without a doubt, inflict horrible karma on ourselves, so we couldn't kill them. Our problem had apparently solved itself and everything was now cool – until the next morning. You guessed it; all the roaches were back in force. It was party time!

We ended up never killing a single roach, and luckily, as far as I know, the kids all survived.

Late one night, not long after the roach episode, we woke up to the sound of a chopper overhead and our house leader yelling, "Eat your stash, eat your stash!" referring to our personal supplies of psychedelic mushrooms. The Tennessee National Guard and the Tennessee State Police were raiding 'The Farm!'

Apparently, a week earlier their 'eye in the sky' chopper that regularly patrolled the state looking for marijuana plants, mistook the neglected ragweed growing in our fields as dope. You can imagine how much love the State of Tennessee had in its heart for fifteen hundred in-your-face hippies!

That night, we had three miscarriages resulting from the commotion with the chopper and all the cops frightening the expectant mothers to death, and the miscarriages devastated them – a miscarriage leaves scars.

Early the next morning, our attorneys, who stopped the invaders at our gate the night before, marched the big shots out into the fields showing them our 'illegal' ragweed, while police and military lined the road outside our gate standing at attention with their rifles and shotguns at the ready. As we slowly drove by in our pickups past the line on our way to Nashville (we were high on mushrooms that really changes you into a five-year-old kid), we just 'happened' to have some ragweed with us that we tossed, like darts, into their gun barrels. Luckily, they just stood there like robots.

The Farm sued the State of Tennessee for a million dollars because of the miscarriages and duress they caused our community, but The Farm never followed through with it. We didn't have the money to pursue it, and we were committed to peace, which took a lot more courage than I thought. I learned how much courage when I witnessed a near tragedy one afternoon while walking toward the gatehouse.

An old pickup, overflowing with nine drunken locals, flew up the dirt road in a cloud of dust and parked just outside the gate. They poured out and ran up to the gatekeeper, a young, thin guy who had been at the commune since its inception. Two of the young men grabbed his long hair and pulled his head back, while another pulled out a large bowie knife and put it to his neck. I couldn't move; it was a horrific sight that froze everybody inside the gatehouse as well. After what seemed like forever, they threw him on the ground, stumbled back to their truck laughing and yelling, and drove off.

We ran up to the gatekeeper and asked if he was okay. He dusted himself off and said that everything was cool and that we should just forget about it.

About a week later, I ran across him in the meadow where the entire community would meditate every Sunday. I asked him if he was scared when they put the knife to his throat.

"Yeah, sure, but they weren't killers, just drunk," he said.

"What did they say?"

"They asked me what I would do if the Russians came and raped my wife and took my kids, whether I would protect them by killing the Russians."

"What did you say?"

"I said that right now there ain't no Russians, just a bunch of good old boys and me, and I was okay with that. Then they said I was worthless and threw me down."

"You're pretty brave," I said.

"Naw, I'm okay with dyin," he said, and then looking down quietly added, "I learned a long time ago how the universe works."

The Farm was a down to earth experience where I met exceptional people like the gatekeeper, and like ten-minute Denny (the walls in our household were paper-thin, acquainting everybody with each other's intimate habits), who was a gifted musician. The three-day night and day concerts that were held every July 11th were attended by the entire community and were remarkable – a meadow of delicate, hopeful faces turned toward the sun with their long hair blowing in the wind like fields of wheat.

Our four professional touring bands and our many amateur musicians provided non-stop music for all the families and kids happily camped out under the stars. It was a great place for kids, and safe, too, with UNICEF keeping an eye on them for any nutritional deficiencies. The only thing they found lacking was vitamin B-12, which we handled easily by supplementing our soymilk.

As great as The Farm was, however, it was idealistic, and it was changing. We began having trouble getting many of the moms to help out, and actually had fifteen acres of tomatoes rot in the fields because nobody showed up to harvest them. Shortly after this, The Farm introduced capitalism.

Previously, all profits from cottage industries went into a pool for the general welfare, and as a result, many individual houses were in dire need of repair. As an experiment to incentivize folks, The Farm decided to allow each adult to go off The Farm one day a week and keep the wages for their personal use. Within weeks, a mysterious, capitalistic energy took over as everyone headed to town to make some extra money, even the moms who would not harvest their tomatoes.

Soon after, The Farm required a police force. Hippies wearing special mono-color T-shirts were scattered about to protect folks from the changes occurring, like the alcohol that was smuggled in resulting in aggressive behavior and abuse. Then there was an un-expected donation and a vote to use the money for either adding a water supply for the folks who lived on the fringes of the property, or getting a dish and cable to feed TV to the entire community. When TV won, I began to understand what the Buddha said about all things eventually changing.

It wasn't long before the October mornings turned cooler and the days a little shorter, and with no real connections for a warm place to stay (since I moved out of the crowded, noisy household, preferring a tent), I decided to return to California.

I had a problem, however. People who take a vow of poverty don't have any money! Nevertheless, I snuck out of the commune one sunny morning and without a penny in my pocket, hitchhiked down the old country lane to Summertown.

You know, as I now look back on my life, the happiest times were when I was penniless. There is something about living on the edge, call it an intensity, a realness, a freedom, or whatever. It's that delicious feeling that we invariably lose in our old age when security becomes more important than discovery.

When I reached town, I brazenly walked into the bank – dirty, sweaty with a full beard, tattered clothes and mismatched socks – and talked the manager into letting me make one collect call, but Janet didn't an-swer. The phone in Lafayette was disconnected.

I only had one more hope before heading back to The Farm with my tail between my legs – that Janet had returned to Shasta Abbey.

The bank manager raised his eyebrows but nodded that I could try again, and when I dialed, I couldn't believe it; a female monk answered (the one that originally kicked me off the mountain when I first arrived at the abbey), and she accepted my call. She said that Janet was living at the Oakland Priory in the Bay Area, an extension of Shasta Abbey, and gave me the number. The banker smiled and permitted me one more call, but no more.

I called the priory and sure enough, Janet was there. She was sick as a dog and in bed with the flu, but immediately wired the bank enough money for a bus ticket back to California.

After I hung up, I took a moment to look into the eyes of the banker. I didn't know if either of us would remember that moment, but there is something so precious about helping others and being helped that beats the hell out of greed in so many ways.

Janet: "I was really sick, but so happy to hear from my best friend forever. He was my rock, my stability, and I couldn't imagine continuing on this journey without him. I knew he would come back to me."

I was a master of escapes. I could pull off simple ones, like losing myself in the music of a summer concert, or even complex ones where I completely surrender myself to someone or something and willing to sacrifice my life for them. Within these precious moments of escape and freedom, my worries about myself would disappear, and I wondered . . . how could I make this freedom permanent without relying on a fleeting cause or a tenuous relationship?

While the bus was sucking up some diesel fuel in one of those non-descript towns where you wonder how people make it, I ran across the highway to a small grocery store praying for some yogurt. Keeping a wary eye on the bus, I hurried in and noticed an elderly couple, maybe in their nineties and old enough to have a hard time getting around. The man was carefully helping his frail wife walk slowly down the grocery store aisle with his arm around her, holding her hand. He was so gentle; a lifetime of shared heartaches and triumphs reflected in his patience. Maybe this was the only adventure they had left, shopping at this little grocery store.

The cashier must have thought I was just another crazed hippie when I stopped in my tracks and right there, in the main aisle, wept unabashedly. How else could I express the loving kindness and compassion that I was feeling? Only at times, such as this, was I able to detect my kindest feelings; only when I took time to recognize the underlying love in others did my relentless antagonism lessen. I couldn't maintain this loving kindness, however, not yet, and soon I would become wrapped up in myself once more.

I loved every mile bussing across this great country, such a vast freedom with so much promise, and too soon, my old dog was crossing the Great Plains, gliding through Salt Lake City and running across the flat, dry salt beds that were surrounded by those majestic Utah mountain ranges. We blew through Reno quickly, and soon the orange smog hanging in the valleys alerted me that we were dropping into California.

It was great being back in the Bay Area, and greater yet to see Janet, the kindest person I had ever known. One day we were walking around downtown Oakland and all of a sudden, she popped the question.

I didn't even hesitate, "Sure," I said, and before we knew it, we were saying our single 'vow' (to help each other find truth in this lifetime) at the Oakland

Buddhist Priory in front of a Zen priest and eight roommates.

Janet: "At that moment in time, I somehow knew that we would continue our 'endless journey' for the rest of our lives. There was no doubt in my mind. Our vow was so heartfelt because finding truth in this lifetime was the only thing that mattered to both of us."

We waved goodbye to the Bay Area and it was now on to Boulder, a small, picturesque town in Colorado surrounded by mountains, and according to some very clued-in hippies at The Farm, a very spiritual place.

We were close to broke after the enormous wedding expenses (two cheap gold rings and a cake) and had to get some money together, but since I was still in exile hiding from creditors, I knew that any job would be short-lived before they tracked me down. We were still climbing mountains of mist.

New relationships, clothes, jobs, houses, towns − holding on, letting go, waiting − for something. We always convinced ourselves that whatever it was we were waiting for was right over that next mountain, but when we scrambled up our mountains and excitedly looked over the top for our deliverance, all we could see was the next mountain.

What were we really searching for? What defining moment started us on this quest? Was it a longing inside, a flash of some kind? Was it curiosity, restlessness, wanderlust? Whatever it was, it was compelling, and it left us no other choice.

Where had I learned my greatest lessons in life? Was it when I was having a good time or when I was blind-sided by disaster? I don't recall many of my childhood birthday parties, but I remember a speeding car running over my little dog and killing him when I was a kid. The memory of my dog convulsing in my arms for a minute or so before he died etched itself indelibly in my mind – and it changed me somehow.

Now that we were married, I found myself torn. I had only been practicing meditation for two years but already the meditation began chipping away at my strong controlling personality, to the point where I began to see past myself at times.

I was the one Janet chose to spend her life with, and I felt responsible for contributing to her happiness and well-being. If I truly believed that there was a next world, and that our present efforts would make a difference of how she fared in that next world, where did my priorities lie?

I thought about the comfortable lifestyle I had with my family. It was fun, and too easy for to me make money, but what does money and family really mean? Security? In the end, can all the money and family in the world help, right after we take that last breath?

How much energy should I devote to Janet's material support and worldly happiness, and how much to her emotional and spiritual development? One would be easy for her; one would be very hard.

Janet: "Ed had no reason to worry about me. I would have followed him to the end of the earth regardless of the hardships, and I would prove that to him soon enough. It's strange how not having much money or worldly possessions didn't bother me at all, maybe because they seemed so insignificant compared to what I really wanted – answers to life."

Boulder was really cool! We found work with a home care agency and got along fine with just bikes and a cheap apartment in a converted motel. On days off, we relaxed either in a park across the street feeding squirrels, or at the Pearl Street Pedestrian Mall that was home to the Boulder Bookstore, a neat refuge where we would spend hours and hours hanging out on the wooden chairs in the aisles.

While thumbing through our favorite spiritual book section one day, we ran across 'Living Buddhist Masters' by Jack Kornfield, an American and former Buddhist monk who had once lived and practiced in Thailand. Were we ready to throw caution to the wind and take a chance overseas? We were standing on a high cliff with untried wings, knowing that we'll never have the chance to fly unless we jump.

Yes! In a flash, we decided to jump! Thailand would not only be an excellent place to deepen our meditation, but a great, untraceable hideout for a fugitive like me. Since we had been meditating seriously in Boulder, we thought that we were ready for anything, so as soon as we accumulated enough funds it was off to enigmatic Thailand and the next adventure for two very naïve nomads who really weren't ready at all for what was awaiting us!

Chapter Five

5. Bubbles in a Stream

Bangkok was teeming. The airport crowd carried us into a cluttered street where frantic cabbies vied for our attention fighting over the scrap of paper in my clenched fist. The most aggressive 'dragged' us into his tiny cab and before I could say, "Where the hell are the seat belts!" he grabbed the piece of paper with '*Train Station*' written in Thai and catapulted us into the worst traffic nightmare in the universe.

The old cab sputtered through the orange, murky air with the driver's bloodshot eyes riveted in some kind of supernatural trance on the kaleidoscope of manic machinery that danced before us. With one hand on the horn and the other flying between the shifter and steering wheel, he launched us into a wall of filthy air and wall-to-wall traffic that could only be described as New York City on steroids. I glanced at Janet – her face was as white as a sheet.

Janet: "This was crazy! This was not driving – this was avoiding head-on collisions every few seconds! Never in my life was I in traffic this risky, and I was glad that I would never have to drive in such danger."

I now realized that this completely nutty idea might have been a mistake. Janet trusted me implicitly, she always had; after all, I was her knight in shining armor! Now, I was risking her life, not only in this insane, uncontrolled demolition derby, but also with what I knew lie ahead. My sheltered, middle class concepts were disappearing like a fading sunset, and I realized that Janet could actually die. I promised myself that I would never let that happen, but our vow to help each other find truth in this lifetime would never be abandoned either. That vow was the only thing that kept me going at times, and I would never back off from it, no matter what.

I badly misjudged our cab driver; he was actually an extremely skilled veteran of the endless bedlam that only begins to describe this untamed city. At least the congestion in Bangkok kept the vehicle speeds down, but out on the rural highways the speed limit was as fast as your car, bicycle, or pushcart could go. It was a no man's land. Accidents were frequent and horrendous with bodies lying all over the roadway like abandoned road kill until local villagers might (or might not) come by and drag them to the side. There were no ambulances in rural Thailand, and very few police.

After an eternity of white-knuckled maneuvering, squealing brakes, and eye-popping acceleration, we lurched to a blessed halt in front of the cavernous Bangkok Train Station. I checked Janet. She was still breathing.

This whole trip began as a pick-up game and things weren't changing. We were running on guts and good luck, or maybe just guts, but at least we had an address. The ticket vendors huddled around the Thai inscription on the post card and after an animated discussion (I wasn't sure if they were excited or incredulous about our destination), they pointed to a line of people across the station. We were yet to discover that the ticket we were about to purchase would take us to the most destitute region of Thailand; the northeast hinterland bordering Cambodia.

At six-foot- two, I towered over the Thais in line who looked up and smiled as if I were some kind of god. Thais had a self-effacing way of making Westerners feel as if we were special and they were nothing, at least back then not long after the Vietnam war when Westerners were still respected. We Americans could be downright arrogant at times, while Thais are naturally gentle and unassuming.

We purchased the tickets and in the process found out how much a Thai 'Bhat' was worth. I had overpaid the cab driver ten times! No wonder he smiled broadly and bowed twice. Oh well, he definitely saved our skin in that traffic, and anyway, we wouldn't be handling money much longer.

We had some time to kill, so we walked to the Bangkok Snake Farm, a great snaky place full of reptile pens and exhibits. We were curious what might *really* kill us out in the jungles. We figured if we could identify the critters that could punch our one-way ticket to an impromptu cremation, perhaps we could avoid them. This is how farangs (Westerners) foolishly thought when they first arrived in 1981 Thailand, as if they still have some control over life and death.

Janet: "I was facing one of my biggest fears in life –snakes! I'm not sure why out of all animals, I dreaded snakes the most, and I felt that I was about to be seriously tested."

I asked the curator what species was particularly dangerous, prompting him to proudly hold up his scarred finger and vividly recount his "oops" with a

Banded Krait that landed him in the hospital for two weeks despite the immediate self-administration of anti-venom. The reality was that we would be far removed from hospitals in the poverty-stricken areas to which we were heading, but of course, we didn't know that yet. We naively believed that medical clinics and ambulances were everywhere, just like home.

We gawked at the snakes and the snakes gawked back, and for some unknown reason I was mysteriously drawn to the large black and yellow rings of the Banded Kraits. Was this a premonition? We studied the identifying characteristics of the Cobras, Russell Vipers, Pit Vipers, Scorpions, and other fierce characters, never imaging for a moment that we would actually come in close contact with any of them.

Janet: "We found out too late that the monastery we were going to was built on land that was vacant for a long time. The villagers would avoid the area because it was overrun by deadly snakes!"

We passed on the recommended inoculations back home because they were expensive and supposedly only effective for six months, so we figured we'd take our chances. After all, we intended to live in Thailand forever. Additionally, we were full of youthful perceptions such as a false sense of security resulting from a basic naivety of the real world.

We were smart enough not to eat in Bangkok, or at least careful of what we ate. We figured that once we arrived at the monastery we would be safe from disease. In hindsight, that was really fogged-over, to say the least. With horror stories of dysentery and typhoid fever dancing in our innocent brains, and all reinforced by Bangkok's open sewers and unregulated, smiling street vendors that obviously were unfamiliar with the word 'hygiene,' we bought a huge stalk of tiny Thai bananas and some Cokes – our breakfast, lunch and dinner. Delicious!

Returning to the train station after our exhilarating romp through Snakeland, we rested for awhile curling up on a wooden bench to await the train. I rolled on my back and noticed insects crawling all over the ceiling towering above us! No . . . wait! These weren't insects at all; they were Thais, so high up that they appeared to be ants. They were working feverishly on the massive, curved ceiling, barely hanging off scanty, lashed-together bamboo scaffolding that swayed dangerously back and forth. Where was OSHA!

Watching the Thais work in these hazardous conditions, I began to feel vulnerable, as if I had been pampered and privileged my entire life and just beginning to wake up to reality. It was a haunting feeling, as if my protected life was about to be undone.

We caught the six-hundred kilometer overnight milk run that was destined to make uncountable stops as it headed to the sparse, destitute countryside of the northeast. Clicking and clacking grudgingly through Bangkok's innards, the ancient train snaked slowly past miles of dilapidated buildings leaning toward the rickety tracks and populated with people surviving on next to nothing. Many of the old and infirm sat seemingly hopeless beside their makeshift dwellings waiting for something, and it made us pause.

We reflected on the fate of all beings, rich and poor, good and bad. Death was the destiny of us all, whether easy and sudden or slow and painful, and we hoped with all our hearts that we would not have to go through the uncertainty of physical existence too many more lifetimes.

Chugging past the squalor of Bangkok and finally heading toward the Cambodian border, we found ourselves gazing out of smeared windows at countless rice fields, their magnificence painted across the endless South Asian landscape. We saw plains dotted with tiny villages framed against a night filled with endless stars, a red streaked morning sky, and a yellow-white day. Eventually these plains gave way to occasional patches of forest, and soon we could see tangled thickets of jungles ahead.

The monastery was supposedly a dozen kilometers from the Ubon train station, but none of the cabbies had ever heard of it. Finally, a slim, young Thai on a tiny motor scooter indicated that he knew where it was and offered to take us there. Great! Except that this was a very small bike, and Janet and I with backpacks must have weighed in at a good three hundred and fifty pounds! The driver was undaunted and somehow squeezed everything on, and with flattened tires, a little luck and a lot of smoke, we soon found ourselves in the forest surrounded by the deafening chatter of tropical, hooked beaked birds.

Janet: "After paying the driver we unloaded our bags and waited at the deserted entrance of Wat Pah Nanachat, a Buddhist forest monastery (wat) established by Ajahn Chah, a famous Thai forest monk. He was one of the Buddhist Masters we read about in Boulder whom had established monasteries all over this remote part of Thailand. This particular one was for Westerners, so most of the monks were from plac-

es like the UK, Australia, the U.S, and Germany."

This was just what we were looking for – isolation! Living in the forest deepened our meditation, something we learned before we were married while living at Shasta Abbey. We saw the jungle, the animals, and the natural world to be fundamentally no different from ourselves; we were connected to the hip with it. We felt safe and comfortable here, even with the dangers that lurked in the forest, but because we understood that, we were no more than merely elements of the earth that would return to the earth, what was there to be fearful of – since we were the earth?

After waiting at the entrance for an hour or so, two monks appeared from inside the monastery. One was smiling broadly, and undoubtedly knew who we were since we had corresponded ahead of time and made the proper arrangements, which was an improvement from our usual, spontaneous pick-up game.

"Hello," he said, his delightful British accent bouncing off the forest. "The Rocks I presume?"

What a friendly, carefree monk! We felt at home already. He got right down to business asking me to remain at the entrance for a moment while he and the other monk escorted Janet to the nun's section. Before they left with her, the British monk asked if I wanted to say goodbye. Hmm. Why should I say goodbye? Janet and I were staying at the same monastery! But I did as he suggested and said goodbye. You should never second-guess a British monk.

I watched her disappear into the trees, which, by the way, happened to be my last personal contact with her for months. I thought back how anxious she was on the motor scooter when she noticed the small, thrown together shelters that farmers used to rest in while working out in the rice fields.

Janet: "I looked out at the rice fields and saw skimpy, straw huts here and there, built on the ground and close to the dangerous snakes that I heard populated the rice paddies. I was scared to death. Would I have to live in one of these?

What a relief when I was taken to the nun's section of the monastery and saw that my first kuti (hut) was made of timbers with a tin roof and perched on stilts for protection against my anticipated despicable critters.

My fears, however, were not entirely unfounded. An active family of foot long lizards (geckos) claimed the hut as well, causing me to lay awake the entire first night. Even though I curled up in a tight, fetal position being careful not to touch the mosquito net that hung from the ceiling, the ends of which I tucked firmly under my little bamboo mat, I couldn't help imagining all kinds of things crawling on me.

Eventually, the nuns gave me a nicer kuti with only two geckos, and later, a new and very beautiful one with only a single lizard, but the lizard was a huge one.

Ed and I would see each other at a distance while attending community meetings and meals, but we weren't permitted to speak with each other without a monk present. These rules were established to prevent misunderstandings with the villagers, who supported these monks, a support that relied upon mutual trust.

The villagers would take care of the monks and nuns' necessities, and the monks and nuns would de-

vote their lives to nothing other than conquering their kileses, (greed, hatred, and delusion) and finding enlightenment. The monks and nuns were the villagers' ideals."

The British monk returned after getting Janet settled in and handed me a traditional small, thin rolled-up bamboo mat that would serve as my sleeping and meditation pad, along with an old, dinged aluminum teapot that was my water kettle.

There was no movement in the monastery, as we walked through the courtyard and approached a large wooden structure in an open area. It was the sala, or meditation hall, about fifty feet by seventy feet and surrounded by five-hundred gallon water barrels placed to catch rain from the tin roof. There was no running water or electricity out here! A bell platform with six steps stood a little way from the sala, and alongside the bell platform was a cremation area. There were enormous windowless openings in the sala shielded from the weather by a wide overhanging roof. The openings were so wide that it appeared as though walls didn't exist; you could look straight through the building as if it wasn't there, an incredible illusion of airiness.

It was peaceful here, but not necessarily quiet. The animal chatter was unending in the forest and changed every hour as the various animals went about their business. They say forest monks can tell time by just listening to the changing noises of the jungle, and I can attest to that; I even got pretty good at it myself!

After a brief stop to fill the kettle at one of the water barrels surrounding the sala, the monk escorted me to the other side of the monastery. While we were walking along, a mangy dog with a missing ear and clumps of absent fur ran into the forest not far ahead of us. The monk pointed to it and issued a stern warning saying that stray dogs from surrounding villages wander about the monastery from time to time looking for food, and that a monk and nun were both presently being treated with anti-rabies shots after being attacked on the porch of the sala. I was relieved to hear that rabies shots were available, but not thrilled about rabid dogs running loose all over the place.

We continued walking about fifty yards on a narrow trail through a green grotto of dense foliage where tropical flowers spilled out of bamboo thickets as if they were welcoming me, and suddenly, there it was; my personal little kuti that I had been picturing in my mind for so long. It looked simply wonderful; quiet, peaceful, and just the thing for an itinerant introvert like me.

It was tiny by Western standards, maybe seven-feet by seven-feet, just enough room to stretch out. It was made of hand cut timbers and perched on four, six-foot high stilts to keep out snakes and floods. Nine steps led to a small porch, and inside were only a few pictures tacked to the wall; an autopsy photo of some poor chap cut from top to bottom, (a typical visual aid monks use to contemplate the body), a picture of a Buddha image, and a picture of a lotus blossom. There was also a small tin can, cut-in-half, that I used later to heat a few spoons of water in, over a candle, to shave with every morning. I only assumed that the previous occupant used it for this purpose as well, and I mentally thanked him for leaving it.

The kuti came complete with two shuttered windows to keep out the rain, and a mosquito net tied to a ceiling beam. Some candles, matches, and incense sat on an interior two by four. Small pans of kerosene were built around the exterior stilts at the bottom of the hut to discourage ants, scorpions and termites, and the roof was covered with beautiful tin where the sound of rain upon it would remain with me for the rest of my life. My little kuti was perfect!

Living at a monastery in Thailand costs nothing, as long as you follow the rules and behave yourself, which included a wealth of cultural things to learn quickly. For example, pointing a foot is akin to exhibiting one's middle finger, so I soon learned to sit 'puppyup,' or flat on the concrete floor of the sala with my feet curled side-saddle underneath. No furniture or pillows were to be found at Wat Pah Nanachat either, only wood, concrete, and the jungle floor.

After the British monk wished me good luck and disappeared down the trail, I glanced around nervously for signs of snakes, mad dogs, or germs before making myself at home in my little kuti with my dinged tea pot that were to me more beautiful than mansions and gold-plated faucets.

The regional police station held our passports, which we gleefully surrendered upon arrival without concern because it was our intention to stay forever. This was paradise, and a rare opportunity to meditate with little disruption.

Janet: "The only chore I had was sweeping my path, which was a meditation in itself. The kindhearted villagers took care of all the food and monastery repairs, allowing the monks and nuns to concentrate on their meditation and training so that they could give wisdom and insight back to the villagers. It was a nice relationship.

The monks here had a certain mystique about them, unmistakable to observe, but difficult to explain. They were hardly noticed, so unassuming and restrained; even childlike in many ways, and our hearts went out to them. This was the real deal, and I wondered if the stories of narrow escapes with death at these wats were exaggerated. I had a funny feeling we were about to find out."

The next morning I noticed a villager along with a monk in the shade of some banana trees, working on a carcass lying on a bamboo table. It looked as if they were skinning an animal. Hmm, I didn't think monks did that. However, as I moved closer I discovered that what they were working on was a human skeleton! Whoa! I thought maybe I should round up Janet and head back to Colorado right now! This was ghoulish; they were actually scraping dried flesh off the bones.

Later that day, overcome with curiosity, along with a sense of the macabre, I ran across a monk near the sala and casually asked him about it. He laughed, agreeing that it certainly might look gruesome, and then told me the story of the skeleton.

The body had been curing in a sealed box under one of the kutis for two years, apparently a necessary step in the process of removing the flesh without damaging the bones. The two years had now expired, so it was time to scrape off the flesh before shipping the cleaned bones to Bangkok for the pinning and bleaching required to assemble a skeleton for display.

He mentioned that during the two years while the body was stored under the hut, monks took turns sleeping in the top portion of the hut for purposes of overcoming their fear of ghosts, and, as expected, had unusual meditation experiences as the body's ghost was believed to roam about the monastery grounds every night looking for its children.

The remains were that of a young woman from the local village. She and her husband, who was now scraping her bones, would come to the monastery regularly to offer food and listen to dhamma talks (sermons). The couple had a little boy, and another child was on the way, and looked forward to a simple life in the village, raising their children and growing old together.

As I listened to the story, it was obvious that this couple wasn't asking for much . . . were they? They were happy with the simplest of things; farming, raising kids, and then dying in the same village where they were born. This was 1981, just before Thailand became 'Westernized' to the extent it is now, and the humbleness and humility of these people back then overwhelmed us time and again. It was a badge of honor for them to have no more than their neighbor had, and if they did, they would share it.

The monk continued his story: After their daughter was born, the woman began experiencing pains that steadily worsened. The pain became so intense and unrelenting that she could only lay curled up in bed all day.

The pain finally became unbearable and she couldn't take it. One night she asked her husband to bring their children to her bed and just hold her. She was saying goodbye.

Her soft crying was not so much from the pain, but from what she was about to ask her husband to do. She wanted to die, the pain was too much; and yet how could she abandon her young children? What would become of them and her husband? Her dreams were shattered. She asked her husband to leave his gun with her.

He refused. How could he do this? He felt ashamed and cowardly that he could not make her better. He wanted to take his gun and rob somebody, and get money to take her to Bangkok, but there was nobody out there to rob; the monks had no money, and neither did the poor villagers.

The woman he loved was in unbearable pain and he was helpless to do anything about it, other than help her kill herself. How could he live with something like that? He would have to kill her himself, and spare her the horror of pulling the trigger.

He couldn't do it; all he could do was to leave the revolver with her and quietly walk out of the hut, unable to look into her eyes. In a few moments, a gunshot rang out.

It was a sad story, and I couldn't help wonder who really pulled the trigger. If she did, was it wrong for her to take her own life? According to the monks, it was, but I reserved judgment myself. How could I know what she was going through unless I stood in her shoes?

I would watch the monk and villager working on the skeleton from a vantage point across the courtyard. Occasionally the small, gentle villager would put his knife down and become silent, looking off into the forest. His lined face and weak smile revealed the pain of a poor villager's life that had come undone, and now he was doing the only thing left to do, fulfill a promise to the woman he loved since they were small children.

Her dying wish was that her skeleton would be displayed in the main hall for the monks to contemplate every day, reminding them that death can come at any time, and therefore they must not tarry in their efforts to find freedom in their hearts, and hopefully not experience death too many more lifetimes.

Janet: "I was amazed to hear that these villagers only had aspirin and some village remedies to help them with their illnesses and pain. I could see that I was coming from a very sheltered life.

I felt so sorry for this woman and the terrible pain she must have experienced, and the horrible things she felt she had to do. Her skeleton hanging in the sala would be a profound reminder of the suffering and uncertainty of life for anyone who would see it.

This poignant story and the actual experience of seeing this skeleton hanging in the hall with a bullet hole in its skull affected me deeply, much deeper than any sermon about us being merely 'bubbles in a stream' that could burst at any moment. I was now actually living the Buddha's words.

The contact with the monks at the Zen monastery in California, our experiences with the monks and nuns here in Thailand, and our deepening meditation all had an incredible impact on this phase of our spiritual lives. Our observation of life expanded into a wonderful perspective, as our worldly appetites fell away and our spiritual faculties began flowering. This created a radical difference in the way we experienced everything, and although we continued circling around life, it was now at a different, more refined viewpoint."

6. Diamonds in Rocks

I retired to my hut for the evening and the next morning, while walking toward the meditation hall, I noticed the abbot standing near the cremation area. He indicated that I should join him, after which he asked if I would help, pointing to a black, tarry lump lying next to a cremation fire that was still in embers. I didn't know what he was pointing at, but of course, I nodded in agreement. I followed his lead and helped gather a good bit of dry wood that we placed on the embers, and after the fire got roaring again, we collected some large banana leaves to protect our hands, after which we carefully picked up the child's hot, small, half-cremated torso and placed it back on the cremation fire.

I reflected on the wide chasm that existed between Thai and American culture, and how mentally tough the Thais must be to live under these third world conditions. When I first arrived I felt sorry for these destitute villagers, but I soon learned that happiness had nothing to do with wealth, comfort or security, and everything to do with courage and a state of mind.

After we placed the body back on the fire, the abbot smiled and said, "You are at Wat Pah Nanachat, and you are now permitted to become a complete failure in the eyes of the world."

What an incredible, liberating statement for a Westerner to hear. I stood there with tears streaming down my face as if a dam had burst. I wasn't sure if placing the infant's body back on the fire triggered the tears, or whether it was the feeling of relief knowing that I would no longer have to live up to a competitive world's expectations. Whatever it was, it freed me. Where was I, exactly? Where have I been all my life?

Thai families would lose as many as half their malnourished children in those days to scores of hazards such as malaria, typhoid fever, and snakebites. The cremation fires stayed busy. The first full cremation I witnessed involved a small girl, six years old perhaps. She was so beautiful, her long, black hair combed so carefully with a pink ribbon tied on the side. She looked as if she were sleeping.

The fire quickly became extremely hot once the branches were lit, and in moments her shiny black hair began sizzling, and then it was gone. Then the skin on her face blistered before it quickly disappeared as well, exposing the white skull underneath. Then the little body blackened, with her limbs curling into a fetal position as she began cooking.

The vivid memory of the episode remained with me for weeks, as the monks warned it would, and it was some time before the skulls that appeared on my kuti wall every evening in the candle light, departed.

Janet: "Neither I, nor any of the other nuns as far as I know, ever saw the cremations. I'm not exactly sure why; maybe because of the impact it had even on the monks. All we ever saw was the embers and the skeletons in the cremation area the next day, and then the relatives collecting the ashes a few days later."

In those days, a cremation area consisted of nothing more than four long stakes pounded into the ground, after which they filled the space with stacks of dry limbs and twigs. The parents would place the body of their child on top of the heap and then stand by stoically watching it burn while the mother threw candy in the air and the father sat on his heals smoking cigarettes and chatting with the men. Expressing emotion was not appropriate etiquette for Thais, and yet at times I caught glimpses of the mothers off by themselves crying quietly. It wasn't considered proper to make a spectacle of yourself.

The villagers appeared to accept these things calmly, while Westerners like Janet and I were horrified, and considered them tragedies. The villagers believed that one's karma determines the length of her or his physical life, and that little could be done to change things. This predestination didn't make sense to our Western minds and our knowledge of medicine, but then, where did my past life experiences at Shasta Abbey in California come from, and where did our other meditation incidents fit into this logical picture?

Deep in our hearts, we had inklings that this universe involved much more than was obvious to us, and now we wondered what was keeping us from seeing this 'more.' Was our strong logic blinding us from seeing extraordinary things that possibly exist outside the range of our limited vision?

Evenings were a welcome relief in Thailand, warm, but without the stifling heat of the day that would grudgingly succumb to the night's coolness. If we weren't in the sala at dusk chanting, or under the abbot's kuti, we would be sitting out in the jungle meditating and hoping to high heaven that a snake wouldn't crawl onto our laps, or a mad dog attack us.

The abbot's kuti was beautiful, surrounded with a profusion of tropical plants and flowers. The hut itself was small, with the actual living quarters not much bigger than a typical hut, but because it was built in the middle of a large, ornate, elevated veranda supported by high, elaborate pillars, instead of the ordinary four by four stilts that propped up our huts, the small kuti had the appearance of being much larger. The Buddha handed down a guideline that huts should be approximately forty feet square, or about six by seven feet, but because the abbot's hut was built on a majestic platform, the structure was large enough so that the entire community could sit underneath.

The abbot would be perched on a seat with one or two senior monks slowly fanning him with giant banana leaves, and except for fierce mosquitoes buzzing around preparing to feast on us, and optimistically not carrying a bad strain of malaria, all was deadly quiet, as the monks would continue to fan their abbot. The humidity was always tangible with the still air hanging heavy and laden with moisture, ready to usher in the monsoon storms during the rainy season. It would be perfectly silent, a powerful silence with these monks and nuns sitting peacefully and not making a sound.

One evening I was sitting under the abbot's kuti, watching Janet across the way and wondering how she and the other nuns were doing, when I noticed a small, brown scorpion crawling up my leg and then continuing onto my lap. I seemed to attract scorpions for some reason as if I had some kind of weird scorpion karma. I just sat there, however, trusting it wouldn't bite me as long as I didn't move . . . hah!

Sure enough, the devious arachnid scurried sideways and with smiling, beady eyes, buried its stinger into my bare wrist. The pain was like ten bee stings all at once accompanied by pins and needles running up and down the entire length of my arm. While I tried to concentrate on my solar plexus to ease the throbbing, the little terrorist just sat there with its tail in the air, looking up at me as if to say, "Have you had enough?" Actually, I had more than enough, and eventually it scurried off leaving me sitting there with thirty minutes of pain contemplation – another one of my many teachers!

Occasionally, the abbot would give a talk. His talks were more or less practical and targeted, centered on our simple struggles to overcome the kilesas – our greed, hatred and delusions that are fueled by our insatiable desires. One evening after a meeting, the abbot invited me to join him in his kuti. As I climbed the steps, I noticed how glossy the handrails and the huge, gleaming floor of the veranda was, a result of his monks energetically polishing the wood with coconut husks until the coconut oil buffed the wood to a deep luster. It was a job that this soon-to-be-ordained novice monk would do on my hands and knees for hours until I got a little too aggressive and ended up on crutches for a week when my old football knee gave way!

The interior of his kuti was much smaller than I had expected. It had the standard two shuttered windows, now open, bare walls, his outer robe hanging on a rack, and near the door sat a water jug, cup, and alms bowl. Except for a few incidentals – a razor, sandals, mosquito net, umbrella and some writing materials – this appeared to be the extent of the abbot's worldly possessions.

We entered the hut to the flurry of two geckos scurrying off the back wall, as the abbot lit a candle and invited me to sit. He offered a cup of water, and then we sat in silence. I felt a profound peacefulness in this man's presence, and already a deep admiration had formed even though I had only known him for a short time. I could have silently sat with him in this little hut forever.

The locusts and cicadas were beginning their evening serenade, beckoning to the pair of geckos that circumspectly made their way to the door to embark on their nocturnal hunt. In the distance could be heard the "gecko, gecko!" of their kinsmen as a soft rain began pattering on nearby leaves – vapors of the earth falling upon the forest to begin their journey back to their source; the great oceans.

The abbot continued sitting quietly without speaking, and I, out of respect, sat silently as well. This man's quiet, sincere demeanor touched me deeply, and no words were needed in this atmosphere of complete confidence and ease. Silence is powerful.

He presently asked how I was doing, I said fine. We talked a little about my practice, the visions I had been having, but then too soon I knew it was time to go. I put my hands together at my forehead and bowed, feeling a genuine respect for this gentle man of few words who accepted me so unconditionally.

Janet and I felt gratefulness and appreciation not only for this abbot, but for the entire group of monks and nuns who willingly gave up the security and comforts of home and family to risk their lives in pursuit of this elusive truth; this unfathomable mystery that held the secret to mankind's only hope. If it wasn't for them and all the other monks and nuns before them that paved the way, how could Janet and I have ever stumbled across meditation.

The rain that began as a trickle was now a torrent. The vast heavens opened their floodgates to unleash angry clouds and storms that drove across menacing, slate-gray skies, and with crashing thunder and blinding lightening as my solitary companions, I returned to my hut.

Traveling to Southeast Asia answered many questions for us; one of them being whether journeying to a distant dangerous place to acquire answers was necessary at all. The answer was yes, because we had always found deep concentration difficult to achieve whenever we were too safe. Danger of some kind, where our lives could be snuffed out any moment, always helped us go deeper.

The wisdom of eternity seemed to rest nowhere but here, within us. Where else could it be? It had always been right here in our hearts but we had always been too busy and full of ourselves to see it. There were those who pointed us in the right direction and helped move us out of our own shadows, but we soon discovered that we must travel this path ourselves until that wisdom surfaced and would forever change our destinies. We were the ones who must make the effort to change because only through our own efforts could we accomplish this transformation.

We never ran across many people who genuinely thirsted for this freedom, and we were beginning to understand why − only a handful of each generation attempted it because it was too difficult. Once, however, that you are cursed by a rare spiritual gene, as we were, there is no going back. All of our bridges, built upon a false security, had been burned.

Our experiences in Thailand so far had already confirmed that what we thought we knew was nothing of value, and a few days later some things happened that we probably would have been satisfied never knowing!

We had been at the monastery for some time when one day we found ourselves boarding the village's only vehicle, a Toyota carryall truck/bus, loaded with a dozen or so other monks and nuns. We were on our way to meet Ajahn Chah, the nationally revered Thai forest monk.

Janet: "I didn't realize what an honor it was at the time to even see Ajahn Chah because I was still young and didn't know much about the advanced, great monks."

As soon as we arrived at the beautiful, well-manicured monastery, an American senior monk straightaway asked me to accompany him into the surrounding jungle. We walked a good distance until he found a particular tree, after which he walked off six paces as if looking for buried treasure. He pointed to a spot on the ground and said, "It would be nice if somebody would carefully dig here." Monks are not permitted to dig in the ground, according to the rules, because they could accidentally kill living beings. They weren't permitted to order others to dig either, but they could suggest.

After finding something with which to dig, I came up with a stout length of bamboo and began digging where he indicated until I hit something solid. Our 'treasure' turned out to be a mason jar.

Similar to specimen jars in hospitals that preserve bits of tissue and organs after an operation, this one also contained dark, round blobs in a murky, yellowish fluid.

I cleaned the dirt off the jar as best I could and handed it to the monk. He carefully opened it, sniffed, and then reached in retrieving one of the blobs and taking a bite.

"Hmm, still not ready," he said, "Here try a bite."

I really didn't even want to get close to whatever it was, but I tried a bite and it wasn't bad, kind of like a salty olive. Then he sealed the jar tightly and said that it would be nice if somebody would bury it again. As I was covering it with loose earth and patting it down, I asked him, "What were those things?" He laughed and said, "Fermented pickled fruits."

"What are they fermenting in," I asked.

"My urine," he replied.

Thus was my rude introduction to the many uses of urine out here, uses with which Janet would soon become familiar.

Ajahn Chah was seated in the sala quietly talking in Thai to a large group of monks surrounding him, as our abbot made his way to the front and said a few words to Ajahn Chah, while pointing in our direction. Ajahn Chah glanced our way, and then said a few words in Thai to our abbot.

"What did he say?" I asked when our abbot rejoined us. He replied, "You can't find a diamond in a rock."

Hmm, mysterious words indeed, with many interpretations; words that have haunted us all these years with their meanings changing as our practice matured.

One of Ajahn Chah's basic teachings went something like this; a longing exists in all of us, but since our wisdom is not complete, we misunderstand this longing. Because we mistakenly believe that the world can satisfy our hunger, we therefore end up in the chicken yard looking for gold, but only pick up the chicken shit!

Janet and I both ordained and soon began appreciating Buddhist training in Thailand. We were taught the basic meditation technique *'anapanasati,'* or watching the breath. We noticed where the incoming rush of air during an inhalation touches the rim or inside of our nostrils, or alternatively if we breathed through our mouth, where the incoming rush of air touched the outer lips or tongue. Then we were to focus gently on that area while at the same time knowing whether it was an inbreath or outbreath that was washing over the area. A senior monk explained it as ocean waves washing over an exposed rock where you would watch the rock constantly, yet be aware whether the breath was an incoming wave or outgoing wave.

I could only focus on my nose tip for a short period of time when I first arrived before my mind would jump around and think nonstop, probably due to our recent traveling. Many times I found myself lost in stray thoughts for a long time before remembering what it was I was supposed to be concentrating on, which was my nose tip and breathing. With the solitude and peacefulness here, however, my meditation quickly improved.

One morning I knew the meditation was improving when the breath, and the nose, disappeared! They were replaced by a still, light-gray screen with no annoying thoughts at all. This screen then became my object of meditation, usually appearing after concentrating on my nose and my breathing for just a few minutes.

Once the screen appeared, time would compress. For example, if the screen appeared at four in the morning, only a few seconds would seemingly go by before it was five-thirty and time to get ready for alms round.

Living in the forest as a Buddhist monk and nun involved an uncommon amount of inward self-sufficiency. Here, our labors were internal, where everything that we had valued externally in the past eventually gave way to this inner purpose. With the support we received here, we now could direct our efforts toward this quest for enlightenment one hundred percent. This was perhaps one of the few places in the world where it was still possible due to the simplicity and absence of complications.

As a nun, Janet had the support of the lay people in the villages even though the support was not up to par with the monks. The upside was that she had less responsibility than the monks did and therefore more liberty to practice. This was good enough for her. She was looking for true freedom, not prestige, and in many ways, the nuns had an easier time of it. They unquestionably had more solitude and less attention paid to them.

Janet: "This was my first opportunity to devote all my time to meditation, and I didn't realize back then how lucky I was. I certainly had a hard time with the course food, however. With only one meal about ten o'clock in the morning and no further food permitted for the rest of the day, I couldn't get enough to eat. At first, the village food was so foreign and coarse that I could only eat rice and bananas, a sure recipe for constipation, and it wasn't long before my bowels stopped dead!

My situation worsened and became critical when I hadn't had a bowel movement for three months. People might find this hard to believe but it was true. I actually wondered why I wasn't dead, or where the little bit that I did eat was going!

In desperation, I finally scrunched up enough courage to speak with the vice-abbot who was known to be a little harsh with whomever he considered to be a crybaby! I tentatively approached him when he was alone in the sala, and he immediately summoned another monk to join us. Two monks must be present when speaking alone with a woman.

After listening somewhat impatiently to my sad story, he exclaimed, "Only three months? I have gone six months without a bowel movement! Don't worry, go drink your urine."

That was hard to hear. Not only was I losing weight and getting very thin, but now I might have to drink my pee as well? I never heard of drinking urine before.

As one could imagine, I tried all kinds of remedies to avoid drinking my urine, but to no avail. So reluctantly, and out of desperation, I finally did as he suggested; I pinched my nose closed, and . . . down the hatch!

Surprise! It wasn't as bad as I imagined, a little salty perhaps, and within a few days of drinking it as soon as I got up every morning, lo and behold – success! As it turned out, I actually preferred drinking my own urine than eating the frogs, insect eggs and grasshoppers, but this episode was only a prelude of what was to come."

While my best-friend-ever was having constipation problems, my tribulations were, as usual, on the opposite end of the spectrum. I awoke one night from a dream where I was sled riding, only to find myself sliding around on my mat! "This is strange," I thought, "what could I be sliding in?" I felt around and it was as if my mat was covered with mayonnaise! I lit my lantern to see what the heck was so slippery, and immediately wished I hadn't. The green, slimy, horrible mess covered the kuti floor, my mat, and me! I was covered in poop. The dysentery came on like a thief in the night and didn't even wake me.

The forest was pitch-black that time of night, the time when many creepy things crawl around, and with no bathroom to clean up in, I had to make my way to an outhouse some distance away where I spent another hour or so squatting in the blackness. Then I took the bottle of detergent that was always available in the outhouses and made my way to the well where I cleaned my inner robe as best I could.

I smelled to high heaven the next morning, wearing the wet inner robe on alms round, but Thais understood these things. I even received more than usual in my bowl that day! The dysentery didn't go away, however. Two weeks later, and still afraid to fall asleep, this nightmare began taking its toll. I became weaker and weaker, and frankly, tired of living in the outhouse, so I finally broke down and reluctantly went to my intolerant-to-those-who-are-sick vice-abbot for help.

Considering my dire plight to be no more than a minor inconvenience out here, the vice-abbot asked a layman to fetch some honey and bananas that he then ordered me to eat for a week – and nothing else!

I did as he instructed and it was great the first day, but boy did I get sick of an exclusive diet of honey and bananas fast, and who in their right mind would believe that honey and bananas could cure dysentery? I certainly didn't. Within a week, however, the honey and bananas did it! My dysentery was cured and I wouldn't have been disappointed never to see a banana or spoon of honey again in my life – or an outhouse!

Then there was the water issue. The sala's roof supplied our drinking water, and this was great during the monsoons of summer, but once the dry season arrived and the rains ceased, the water in the barrels became less than pristine with various dead, rotting creatures floating about. There was no bottled water in those days!

To supplement the little disease makers in the barrels, the Thai women would religiously wash their fruits and vegetables with the yellow, brackish water from typhoid ridden shallow wells that were fed from the surrounding drainage.

About the surrounding drainage: The monks (and nuns?) would urinate into four inch diameter hollow bamboo tubes inserted into the ground, and guess where the urine wound up after it soaked into the ground – yep, the wells where our food was washed.

To defecate, small enclosures similar to outhouses were scattered about with just a hole in the ground, and guess where that all ended up, too!

Squatting over a hole in an outhouse was a very natural way to relieve oneself because compressing one's intestines with one's thighs works much better than a standard western toilet with a high seat.

The absence of toilet paper was also an advantage.

A squirt-bottle filled with a mixture of dish soap and water did a better job of cleaning one's buns than smearing paper all over them. Toilet paper also clogged the drainage systems and required digging more holes and moving the outhouses more often. The idea of the detergent bottle was to squirt wherever one needed it and then use one's fingers, of the *left hand* (always the *left hand*), to tidy up a bit.

Monks ate with their hands. Utensils for eating such as forks, spoons, knives, or chopsticks were frowned upon, so monks were always careful to eat with their *right hand* (always the *right hand*). Sometimes I would get my hands mixed up and inevitably come down with something, and boy did I ever, regularly!

Chapter Seven

7. The Rabbit in the Moon

It came on fast one morning when somewhere between my kuti and the sala my legs suddenly buckled. I made it back to my hut before collapsing on the floor, and there I lay for two weeks staring at the ceiling and exploring the reality of typhoid fever (which a monk more or less confirmed when he brought me some food) in a forest monastery.

Perhaps it was the meditation, or maybe no longer feeling responsible for anything since I was now hidden away in this forgotten land, but whatever the reason, I oddly didn't fear death at all. Whether I died or lived was of no consequence whatsoever. In the States, it was different. I was important, very important, at least in my mind. I had to make a living and had things to accomplish, and I couldn't afford to be ill. And death? Well, that was unthinkable. Now, however, I was no more than a small part of nature, a tiny part of the earth, and an even tinier part of the countless universes.

Lying on the floor with no distractions and in complete solitude day after day, I had time to ponder the cells and chemical compounds, the water and gasses — everything that I was made up of, and I realized that it all came from the earth and would someday return to earth as well. The natural cycle of life and death was never as evident as it was in this jungle. Life and death happened, every moment right before my eyes.

The village doctor stopped by one day, I assume on

orders from the abbot, and gave me the routine Thai physical that consisted of a handful of red pills (always the same red pills regardless of the illness) and a smile. I appreciated the smile, but never took the pills. I wondered what they were and guessed some kind of shotgun antibiotic that supposedly cured everything!

I definitely experienced a sense of fearlessness during this bout with typhoid, and even though I was extremely weak and feverish, I felt no apprehension at all. Every morning a fellow monk would look in on me and bring a bowl of food and a kettle of water. Their kindness was, of course, shown by feeding me and looking in on me, but more than that, they gave me space to be alone with illness – a profound teacher, and I would not have traded the experience for anything, no matter how dire it was.

Typhoid hit Janet hard, much harder than it hit me, and when the vice abbot actually became concerned enough to pay her a visit at her kuti, she knew she was in trouble. With furrowed brow, he suggested she take some medication, but warned that villagers who took Western medicine for typhoid usually died, while those who took their own village prepared concoctions survived.

Janet always had problems making decisions, she agonized over the silliest of things, but this time, it was far from silly. She was a Westerner and trusted Western medicine, but she trusted the opinions of this abbot as well. What to do? Finally, being the feisty soul that she was, she chose the village medicine and lived to tell the tale. She was up and around again after about a week.

Janet: "I remember lying on a platform under-

neath my kuti, not worrying or feeling like I was going to die but just waiting to get better. Nothing seemed to faze me."

Just when Janet thought that she had cheated death once more, death reminded her who was boss out here. Unknown to her, deadly snakes had crawled into the upper interior roof supports of her kuti and remained hidden until one day she noticed one of them move near the ceiling just as she was about to enter the hut. Then it was a scramble to get away from the hut and holler for help. After a few of these terrifying episodes where the nuns raced to her rescue, some villagers kindly removed the snakes from her kuti and trimmed the overhanging trees so the snakes could no longer drop onto her roof.

Janet: "Although typhoid didn't bother me, the snakes were something else! I was finally facing one of my biggest fears in life when I walked up the steps to my kuti, as usual, and saw my first snake in the rafters. Luckily, I looked inside before entering! I didn't take any time to see what kind of snake it was, I just ran down the steps as fast as I could and yelled for help.

Two more times I had snakes in my kuti and was surprised when the abbot said that no one had ever had a snake in their kuti before! I had always kept my eyes glued to the paths whenever I walked, but now I had to inspect my entire kuti constantly because I found them on the floor as well!

Occasionally, a King Cobra would find its way into the women's outhouse at night, and only the ability to grow eyes in the back of my head kept me alive at times. I had many interesting adventures, including losing a lot of weight that I couldn't afford to lose, but eventually I was able to stomach a little of the village food and regain my health. One of my nun companions was not so fortunate.

My two companion nuns were from China and the UK. The Chinese nun was robust and full of energy, but the British nun, who had been in Thailand for some time, was very thin and sickly. When she finally did return to the UK, it was discovered that she was harboring a number of serious diseases, including malaria."

I can't begin to say enough about Janet and these gritty nuns. When others might have given up and ran home at the first inconvenience, they never complained. Janet remained true to our vow regardless of her difficulties, because she, too, had genuine courage.

Janet was never bitten by a snake or a scorpion, but unfortunately I wasn't that lucky! The rules were that we never wore sandals inside structures or on our alms rounds into the villages, which made the rough gravel roads an interesting study in pain! Therefore, we walked barefoot mostly, only occasionally wearing flip-flops.

One early morning in the shadowy darkness just before the dawn, I was doing some walking meditation in the back of the sala when I felt as if I had stepped on a hot nail! I had no doubt that a snake had crawled into the sala and whacked me.

It was still pitch-black outside with only dim candles lighting the hall, so I scrambled for my lantern that was sitting on the raised platform. I hurriedly lit it and looked around for the snake, hoping that it had not crawled off so that I could identify it. The pain was unbelievable. Then I saw it in the middle of the floor. The little brown rascal wasn't a snake at all – just a scorpion standing its ground in attack posture glaring at me and daring me to try to step on it again. That was not going to happen – at least not in this lifetime!

The abbot came over and waived one hand in front of the terrorist to distract it while slowly reaching behind with his other hand, grabbing it by its stinger and thus disarming it. He tossed it back out into the forest where it belonged, while I went back to my walking meditation with a familiar object to contemplate – scorpion pain – that cool combination of severe stinging and intense pins and needles up and down my entire leg.

We all had duties at the wat and I was no exception. I was given the traditional newcomer's task of ringing the large bell every morning at three a.m., meaning that the poor bell ringer had to make sure he woke up before everybody else. I anticipated no problems, however, and promised myself to ring the bell without fail. The bell was located next to the sala on a raised platform near the cremation area. This was going to be great. I envisioned myself ringing the bell and watching glowing skulls at the same time while alone out there in the middle of the night.

After I was given my new bell ringing responsibility, I was walking back to my hut and noticed that indeed the leaves do pile up this time of year; the path was almost covered. I was tired, however, and decided to sweep the long path the next afternoon notwithstanding a very subtle nagging in my heart telling me to do it now. It was that silent voice I was not completely in touch with yet, a tiny voice that more often than not became a loudspeaker.

I threw myself into meditation that night, worried that if I did fall asleep I would not wake up in time to perform my duty. Even though I set two clocks, I dreaded the thought of accidentally sleeping through the alarms and being responsible for all the monks sleepily arising mid-morning and missing alms round. I didn't know that monks have built in alarm clocks and can awaken at whatever time they wish, and furthermore, many stayed up all night meditating and didn't require being woken up at all!

Finally, three a.m. approached, so I lit my dim kerosene lantern and began walking toward the hall. I could barely make out the path in the darkness because of the thick layer of leaves, again reminding me to sweep the path later that day without fail.

After stumbling along for awhile, I glimpsed a leaf moving about six feet ahead of me. For some odd reason I stopped and looked closer and there under the leaves were black and yellow rings sliding by. Had I stepped down, I would have found myself on the wrong end of a Banded Krait, and that surely would have ended me.

Even though some monks carried vials of village-prepared anti-venom and needles in case of snakebite, the remedy was neither conventional nor very effective. Puncturing the head and shoulders of the snakebite victim with hundreds of needle pricks and then rubbing in the anti-venom, after which the stricken monk would retire to his kuti until he got better or died, was not exactly within proven medical modality.

We somehow survived the months that went by

with one day melting into another and each much the same as the last, as we fell into a delightful daily routine. After ringing the bell and lighting the candles in the sala, I would join the other monks and nuns sitting together practicing meditation until dawn when a senior monk stepped outside to look at his hand. Being able to see the lines on his palm in the gathering light would be the signal for us to put on our outer robes (sanghatis), place our bowls in our slings and begin walking to the surrounding villages to accept food from the villagers. The timing would get us there at sunrise when the villagers expected us and would be waiting outside their huts ready to place food in our bowls.

I would join a small group of monks that had a route across some fields toward the east and the rising sun where we would pass rice paddies with countless pit vipers, both in the water and on the banks, craning their bodies and flicking their tongues to smell what was coming. Mango and banana trees speckled the landscape, as a floating red ball danced on the horizon every morning to greet us monks walking in silence and concentrating on our meditation with heads bowed.

Our walk to the village and back would begin in the forest past orchids and blossoms of every description. Colorful birds frolicked in the trees while tiny barking deer and large eared squirrels busily scurried along the ground while pungent odors oozed out of the clacking bamboo groves. Large feathery ferns would accompany us until we crossed the rice fields and then approached the village down a narrow lane that was fenced on both sides.

Water buffalo tied underneath villagers' dwellings

would cast wary eyes, lowering their heads in annoyance as we approached. Whether our presence reminded them that soon they would be led to the rice paddies for a day of toil, or whether they just didn't much care for orange colored robes was immaterial, the fact was; they didn't like monks!

One morning we were walking peacefully along the lane with our heads down and in single file, when we heard something that sounded like thunder! When the 'thunder' was accompanied by frantic shouting, our heads-down suddenly went to heads-up in a flash! Barreling around the corner at full speed directly toward us were two gigantic water buffalo looking very much like two humongous gray freight trains just a few seconds away.

With no time to think, we leaped over the fence as gracefully as if we were Olympic high jumpers, with robes, bowls and everything else flying as the buffalos thundered down the path followed by their frantic owner who was trying to run, bow, and apologize at the same time. The owner eventually caught up with his animals and came back to check on us, apologizing profusely while we unceremoniously dusted ourselves off and tried to look as dignified as possible climbing back over the fence.

The villages were full of activity. Dogs, some of them infected with rabies, ran wild in the streets, while smiling mothers stood outside their huts washing their babies by holding them up in the air with one arm and throwing cold buckets of water on their naked, chilled bodies. The villagers would stop their activities for a moment with their hands together when we walked by out of respect for the monks who had dedicated their lives to the higher ideals.

I glanced back at one of the mothers one day. She was happy within this precious snapshot of her life. Who in the many worlds could be more content than this impoverished villager and her baby in that moment? What wealth and power could offer her more happiness than she was feeling in that small village?

Further down the lane a group of villagers would be waiting with small, assorted baskets of delicious looking sticky rice, bananas, mangos and coconuts followed by not-so-appetizing baskets of grasshoppers, insect eggs, lizards, snakes and dried fish. Thankfully, final baskets of splendid honey cakes and other goodies saved the day.

We walked slowly in single file with heads bowed as each villager placed some food in each of our bowls. Since I was the newest monk, I unfortunately was the last in line. That means that I was the prime target of the rabid dogs that always chased the last monk as dogs chased pickup trucks back home, and these were no cuddly foo-foo dogs; these were more like ugly hyenas with foaming mouths! Maybe I imagined the foam.

Returning from the villages, we would gather in the sala and sit on a raised platform against the wall. After we were seated, the farmers would walk past and add things to our bowls, things that I particularly didn't relish, but how could I turn down the farmers smiling faces as they offered us the raw insect and fish eggs that would have provided their kids with precious protein that they needed.

What saved me from the raw insect eggs was the 'dhutanga monk' practice of stirring everything together in one's bowl before eating, mixing the insect eggs with the honey rice cakes and everything else.

This supposedly prevents a monk from dwelling on the sensory delights of food and from making choices about which foods he prefers that would bring up thoughts of greed, craving, and a lust for the goodies. But for me, mixing everything together in the bowl had only one benefit; disguising the insect eggs!

I fell into a daily routine beginning with walking to the bell platform at three a.m., ringing the bell and lighting the candles in the hall. With the cremation area strategically placed close to the bell platform, I was able to contemplate the hot skulls lying in the glowing embers from previous cremations. At times, in those dark morning hours, I was positive that the skulls were smiling at me, but of course, it must have been my imagination; how can a skull smile? Or are they always smiling?

Another occurrence was stranger yet. After ringing the bell, I would enter the pitch-black hall to light the candles. There, in the lantern's dim glow, the 'baby' would immediately draw my attention. When it died in infancy, the parents chose not to cremate it and instead donated its body to the wat so that it could be displayed in the hall. It floated in a large, transparent jar filled with some kind of liquid, perhaps formaldehyde, as if it were sleeping with its eyes closed. The baby, who had hair on only one side of his head, was intended to be a warning to the monks that they had better be diligent in their practice because life was a mere bubble in a stream that could burst at any time, even in infancy.

There was something even stranger about this baby. Whenever I entered the dark sala in the wee hours of the morning to light the candles, I could swear, at first glance in the dim glow of my lantern that it was

staring at me with its eyes wide open! This was unnerving to say the least, but the instant I swung
around to look directly at it, its eyes would be peacefully closed as usual. Like the smiling skulls, however, I merely chalked it up to my imagination.

Once the bell was rung and candles lit, monks and
nuns would start filing into the hall to practice together from three thirty in the morning until dawn, at
which time we would begin walking silently into the
surrounding villages in bare feet and with bowed
heads. The only excuse for missing alms round was if
a monk was fasting or ill. Various monks were always
fasting to improve their meditation and would not
make the trip into the village, preferring to remain in
seclusion for sometimes weeks at a time only drinking
water and fruit juice in the afternoons.

At times, illness would prevent a monk from not
showing up for the morning's meditation. In this case,
they remained alone in their huts with their malady
until they either improved or died. The abbot would
usually override the monk's wishes to gamble with
death, and insist that the village doctor stop by if the
abbot thought the illness was life threatening. The
monks viewed illness as an excellent opportunity to
go deeper and realize for themselves that birth was to
be avoided, because birth was a sure recipe for untold
suffering.

*Janet: "The sutras say that the Buddha, as a young
man, was shielded from this suffering of humanity by
his father who insisted that he not go out among the
common people and remain in the three palaces that
his father provided for him. He, however, snuck out
anyway and saw in the streets examples of an old*

man, an ill man, a deceased man, and a monk.

The Buddha didn't have to look any further to rec-
ognize the danger of birth and the advantages of nev-
er being reborn again – what the monks and nuns
were trying to do. This, right here, is what his father
was afraid of – the Buddha becoming a monk instead
of a monarch.

These brave monks and nuns at the wat had no fear
of death and considered death merely a transition,
another opportunity to seek truth. They didn't see life
as a beginning and ending, but saw it as a continua-
tion."

After alms round, we would return to the hall about
ten in the morning and eat our one meal of the day in
silence, after which the abbot would give a talk, and
interact with any villagers who remained to discuss
personal, village or monastery affairs.

When we finished eating, we would wash our
bowls in a nearby stream, dry them, and leave them
on the grass for a few minutes tipped toward the sun
to dry, before returning to our huts to rest and practice
meditation. This is when I did most of my sleeping so
that I could later sit in meditation most of the night
when it was cooler and my meditation was deepest.

At four in the afternoon, we would sweep our paths
before meeting up by the well where we would bathe
and occasionally sit around making bamboo brooms
for path sweeping or washing our robes and dying
them with Jackfruit bark. This was a social time as
well where we might have a fruit drink and discuss
our meditation or anything that might have come up
in the community or in the villages, but I was careful
not to chat mindlessly, which could wreck my medita-

tion for days. Some monks stayed away from social meetings completely just for this reason.

Occasionally I would meditate in the sala or sometimes out in the jungle in the evenings where increased challenges awaited such as curious snakes looking for a warm lap to curl up in! I couldn't believe that I actually was becoming fond of danger after my bout of typhoid. Danger and fear, even pain always deepened my meditation by keeping me alert.

I loved severe thunderstorms, too, with its blinding lightning crashing all around my kuti. Amazingly, no monk or nun, to my knowledge, was ever killed by the storms, although there were some close encounters when trees fell on kutis, crushing them. Interestingly enough, this occurred when the monk or nun was elsewhere. Good karma?

Many nights I sat under an immense canopy of stars casting a silvery-white glow that suffused the entire forest. It was dazzling out here in the pristine non-electrified, silent countryside. I loved to gaze at the brilliant moon playing in a deep, black sky that busily spewed out its myriads of diamonds, and where only the sounds of the night creatures could be heard. What precious moments! I would look for the 'rabbit in the moon' that the villagers were always keen to point out, and which became my silent friend.

In the moon's soft glow, I could make out ants forming bridges on leaves with their bodies enabling the rest of the colony to walk from leaf to leaf. The ants reminded me of the monks and nuns who were forming bridges for Janet and me as well, and sometimes I would find myself struggling to hold back tears.

Something in the jungles of Thailand went directly

to my heart. I couldn't discern it with my intellect, but my heart felt it, and I found myself becoming emotional quite often. This level of reverence was rare, such as that one brief moment at Shasta Abbey when the morning sun glinting on the pine needles triggered such awe and wonder.

Many things wound their way through the night's mysteries including wide trails of aggressive army ants. Stumbling onto an army ant trail insured numerous excruciatingly painful stings in a matter of seconds as they swarmed up one's legs.

Small creatures accidentally wandering onto one of the deadly paths would be covered with ants like a moving carpet within moments, as it desperately tried to escape, but soon the small creature would stop moving as the ants began dismantling it.

Watching these life and death dramas unfold night after night made me realize that every creature, animal or insect, treasures and fights for its life. This awareness, once hidden in the recesses of my mind, now momentary flashed in a way that enduring insights usually do; they change people. This particular flash, and there were many, permanently instilled within me a deep-seated resolve to protect life; a resolve that I felt would remain unshakable no matter how many lifetimes I would endure.

My old tendencies were slowly changing as these flashes of insights, enabled by a calm still mind, dropped from my head into my heart. That's how meditation seemed to work for me; nothing much happening until one day I saw something that I might have seen a thousand times before, but this time it penetrated, and my very being was transformed.

One evening I was watching a colony of red termites locked in death grips with a colony of tan termites. The opposing colonies were on the move and accidentally happened to cross each other's paths, resulting in a war. I wondered why they simply didn't go around instead of killing each other, but of course, how could I expect termites to understand when humankind acted no differently?

The things that we were experiencing in Thailand confirmed that we knew little about the reality of the world, and later things happened that we would have been satisfied never knowing.

At this moment in time, however, watching termites at war with each other at Wat Pah Nanchat, I couldn't help wonder what in the world I was doing here. I didn't know at the time that this was only the beginning of an incredible lifetime of discovery.

I no longer needed books. The jungle, the animals and the creatures became my teachers, and whenever I was able to touch the stillness that was inside of me during meditation, the wisdom of the universe became my teacher.

Chapter Eight

8. Never Say You're Sorry

Time passed quickly at Nanachat and it wasn't long before I became fearless, certain that I could do anything or go anywhere and still retain the insight that I developed during my stay here. My wings that were once broken now soared, to the extent that one day I convinced myself that Janet and I were ready to jump out of our secure raft of Wat Pah Nanachat and swim the river of life on our own until we reached that far shore.

Janet: "I had misgivings about leaving Wat Pah Nanachat because the monks were living a life much the same as the Buddha did twenty-five-hundred years ago, and it was authentic and wonderful.

Shasta Abbey 'saved' my life and introduced me to the basics of Buddhism and meditation, but the actual experience of living the original Buddha's path, fraught with dangers here in Thailand, was an extraordinary sobering and maturing process.

While the abbey, which is Mahayana, included many ceremonies and related to Buddhist saints who lived with the Buddha or appeared after he died, they didn't talk much about the Buddha himself.

Wat Pah Nanachat, which is Theravada, teaches through the Buddha's actual sermons and words, and has fewer ceremonies that are mostly restricted to monk and nun ordinations.

What was good at the abbey was the emphasis on meditation, whereas the Thai Theravada tradition re-

lies more on the discipline of the monks and nuns, and with the exception of a few teachers, pretty much leaves the question of meditation up to each person.

However, for the Thai Theravada monks and nuns who go deeply into meditation, the Buddhist suttas explain in detail the jhanas, deep states of meditation mentioned in at least forty percent of all the thousands of pages of Buddhist suttas that the Buddha taught. Jhanas, according to the Buddha, was meditation. In Thailand, however, these jhanas are rarely mentioned.

Typically the meditation that is taught in Thailand consists of two steps. The first step is practicing breath meditation until the mind becomes 'calm' (this is technically the second jhana but Thai teachers usually don't mention jhana or the finer points of jhana). After the mind becomes calm, then the meditator is trained to investigate the insides of the body. This training is called 'samatha/vipassana.'

The abbey never mentioned these jhanas, at least not to new monks and nuns. Perhaps they considered the jhanas to be more advanced teachings and reserved them for more experienced monks and nuns.

At the abbey, meditation training consisted of 'just sitting,' or 'Shikentaza.' This 'emptying of the mind' therefore did not require any detailed analysis, only the patience to sit for a long time and let the mind empty itself. Very little technique was involved. It was basically watching the mind work and then letting it go – letting thoughts dissolve by themselves until there was just emptiness. This would correspond to a 'first jhana' that occurs after the breath disappears and during an experience of a 'nimitta' or bright light in the consciousness, and great rapture.

As an old Zen master once said, however, "Comparisons are a disease of the mind." Therefore, I am just so grateful that I had a chance to experience both traditions. They were invaluable to me."

I was dead wrong, of course. This idea to take off on our own was no more than spiritual immaturity and simple restlessness. Somewhere, deep in my silent heart, I felt terrible for my lack of wisdom and the mess I was about to make, but my logic and conceit rode roughshod over any inkling of wisdom that was stirring. Logic and conceit whispered to me, "Never admit you're wrong – and never say you're sorry."

Serene mornings sitting together in the hall, the walks to the villages, the days we gathered to dye our robes, and the full moon nights where we would immerse ourselves in meditation – these memories would remain forever.

The monks at Nanachat nursed our bodies and our spirit. They fed us honey and bananas for dysentery and convinced us to drink our own urine to cure other maladies. The solitary life of these monks and nuns were destined to leave few footprints on this earth and make little karma through their selfless actions and peaceful existence but the footprints they left on us were immeasurable.

Perhaps the quality that rang so true with these monks and nuns was that nobody was home. No 'self' was to be found. Their outward attention, always directed toward others, saw themselves no differently from whomever or whatever arose in their consciousness.

It was now time, however, for us to go off on our

own again, foolishly thinking that the world was our oyster and we could do anything, go anywhere and carry Wat Pah Nanachat's protections with us. Instead of turning the incredible confidence we developed inwardly through meditation, we were still spiritually immature enough to foolishly turn this confidence outwardly, and waste it on the world.

Our passports were finally returned by the police, and after spending three days being escorted around Bangkok by an army officer to make sure we left the country, we headed home. The flight had a glitch, however; our departure in Bangkok was delayed. This caused us to miss our connection in India, that shouldn't have been a problem except that when we arrived in New Delhi, we were escorted off the delayed flight and taken to a local police station by soldiers sporting automatic rifles! Was it our bald heads? Was it a miscommunication from the suspicious army officer back in Thailand? This was weird.

After being questioned rather roughly, we were left sitting in a green, featureless interrogation room with the door locked. I thought for sure that we would never see the good ol' States again. We weren't drug dealers or money launderers – honest!

After what seemed like an eternity, the door opened, and things got progressively worse – we were shuffled into a waiting car instead of a cell. Oh great, this was scary. At least we would feel some semblance of security in a cell at the police station, but now where were they taking us – to a wooded area to rub us out?

We drove an interminably long time, finally winding through a wealthy area before pulling into what appeared to be the Taj Mahal. After they checked us in, we were taken to a palatial suite with gold plated faucets – the exact opposite of our little kutis in the forest! The next morning, a knock on the door escorted us back down to the lobby where a police car took us directly to the airport. The two officers bypassed everybody in the ticket line, moved us to the front, helped us make our connecting flight, and made sure we got on the plane.

To this day, we have no idea what happened in India. Our best guess is that we were suspected of something, who knows what, and then the police, discovering that it was a case of mistaken identity or bad information, shuffled us out of India before we could complain to the American embassy. Whatever happened, it was a relief to lift off the tarmac. We had to admit, however, that we experienced very special feelings while in India that went far beyond the mere circumstances of a near police bust, and we have always wanted to return.

Janet: "With little money and no place to stay, my sister and brother-in-law were kind enough to take us in. These generous folks always welcomed us, looking past our bald heads and inviting us to stay with them whenever we needed help. At the time, they were developing a small oil field on a beautiful, remote piece of property in Pennsylvania where we could stay free in trade for taking care of the wells, and an interesting phase in our journey was about to begin."

The property was stunning, with beautiful, pristine hardwood forests on a one-hundred-acre hill overlooking the valley. While Janet's relatives stayed in an old, century home on the Allegheny River five miles down the road in the charming tourist town of Tionesta, Janet and I chose to live on the property in a tent.

The tent idea worked well until brown bears started visiting us in the middle of the night looking for goodies, so a used mobile home was set up for us on the hill overlooking the valley and affording us a spectacular view. Our picturesque reprieve was to be short-lived, however.

We spent delightful days walking through shoulder high goldenrod, picking wild blackberries and rasp-berries, and occasionally running across brown bears with their cubs in the patches. The bears were more playful than dangerous, surprising us by suddenly standing up in the goldenrod as we walked a few yards away, or smelling something good in the kitchen and banging on the mobile home in the wee hours of the morning. Fox, deer, rabbits, raccoons, possums and signs of cougars kept us company, as did the Milky Way at night that seemed to stretch like fairy mist across an endless sky enveloping our campfires.

Before we knew it, however, bulldozers were cutting roads through the hardwoods and stacking huge piles of logs that would be our future winter firewood, and although it was exciting, we had serious misgivings while watching the dozers cut down the beautiful trees.

Our time on this hill was precious. We cut firewood for our woodstove, made homemade bread, pressure cooked soybeans, ran the three-wheeler around that was purchased to tend the wells, and meditated hours upon hours. It was all very conducive to uninterrupted seclusion and insight.

Taking meditation into our daily lives was happening naturally. We were finding that the coming and going of our life situations was merely a mirror of the ever-present thoughts and moods that flitted by in meditation, and found ourselves observing life no differently than we observed our ephemeral breath during practice.

Before we knew it, our idyllic life was jarred by drilling and fracking rigs getting bogged down in the spring mud and later running up and down the newly cut-in roads, popping in oil wells every couple of acres. Janet and I helped where we could, but frankly, we were more interested in digging up a plot of ground next to the mobile home for the hundred tomato plants we were nursing in their little boxes.

The first three wells went in close to the mobile home, not only ruining our water well but also leaving behind pump jacks that we discovered were giant lightning rods, and we were in for it since we lived on a hill! Although lightning never hit the trailer, it regularly hit the pump jacks, making the severe storms that frequent northwest Pennsylvania interesting to say the least.

Once a well was drilled, steel pipe casing was run down the hole and pressure introduced by huge fracking rigs. These rigs would shatter the rock strata below, allowing the oil mixed with salt water to seep from the formations. Rods with seals would be lowered into the casing and then pump jacks, looking like giant grasshoppers, would bring the saltwater and oil mixture to the surface. Underground plastic piping was run from the wells to large storage tanks in the middle of the property where the oil and salt water would be separated. The oil would be stored in the tanks until a local distributor picked it up, while next

125

to the tanks a large, deep pit was dug and sealed with plastic sheeting to hold the salt water until it could evaporate.

As the wells were completed, my job was to make sure that each well was pumping twice a day for an hour or so on a rotating basis. This involved all kinds of electrical and mechanical maintenance on pump jacks that were routinely damaged by lightning.

In time, however, Janet and I became disheartened. Things that initially endeared us to the property were changing, as all things do, and sadness was creeping in. One day I looked at the creek that ran through the property and realized that everything in it, all the frogs and fish and water spiders were dead. The salt water had leaked out of the holding pond and contaminated the ground water coloring it a telltale red. With many old trees being cut down to make room for the rigs, the land was beginning to erode, and the pump jacks were rusting away as well.

I found myself becoming emotional quite often. I felt as if I was standing on a tarmac tearfully waving goodbye to a dear friend that I knew I would never see again, and although the pain was melancholy, it was painful nonetheless.

Janet: "The time we spent by ourselves on this little hill was precious. The work was uncomplicated and we were pretty much shut off from the world with no electricity and just propane and a wood stove.

Unlike monasteries where there are typically many people, this was a chance to be really in solitude. It was so easy to get the mind relaxed and into sitting meditation which we practiced for many hours a day.

However, now it was time once more to surrender supports that we relied upon, and whenever we did this, we would often find ourselves navigating through turbulent waters. This always left us no foothold, but maybe this was exactly what we needed in order to slide down that mountain we had created and had been struggling to climb. If need be, we were willing to live again in both material and spiritual poverty."

It was now time to leave our little hill, and like two rivulets of rain running into a stream that is happily returning to its source, we ended up at the Zen Center in San Francisco.

Thinking that I had immunity against any kind of serious illness, I threw myself into the practice, but I was about to learn that what I 'thought' was my destiny, seldom was.

It happened on the second day of a weeklong, fourteen-hour a day intensive meditation retreat. I was sitting peacefully in the meditation hall with my practice being positively influenced by the subliminal effects of about forty other monks and lay people in the hall.

My 'blank screen,' that first appeared in Thailand, had now been replaced by a light between my eyes, which I found interesting – until that second day of the retreat.

As I sat in the zendo absorbed in the light, large blocks of time began to disappear from my awareness. The bell would sound, indicating the beginning of a forty-minute meditation period, and seemingly, two seconds later it would sound again ending the session, similar to my experience of time disappearing in Thailand. The experience was intriguing, and somewhat amusing, until unexpectedly in the hall that afternoon, everything changed forever.

It began with a literal, audible 'bang,' as if a lightning bolt had struck me. I actually thought that someone had snuck up behind me and hit me on the top of the head with a heavy book. Immediately afterwards, I heard booming words coming from a loud speaker, "*You are now completely healed.*" The words, however, were not coming from a loudspeaker; they were coming from my mind.

This kind of experience was totally foreign to me – words so powerful and commanding that they etched themselves permanently in my brain. This, however, was only the beginning.

My ears began ringing, a high tone, and a very low tone at the same time, while the upper part of my body became very warm, almost feverish. I also felt astonishingly free from every restraint and became extremely giddy because of it. I could barely control the urge to laugh out loud and actually thought that I would have to leave the hall before I disrupted everyone.

At the same time, I envisioned waves of energy flowing from the top of my head, down through my body and out the bottom of my feet spreading throughout the hall and into each of the silent meditators sitting with me.

I had to fight to keep from laughing. How silly my fellow meditators looked, sitting there practicing their meditation with such seriousness and concerned faces. I also wanted to laugh at those powerful words that blasted from inside my head, "*You are now completely healed.*" Healed of what? I was in peak physical condition, the prime of my life! What needed healing?

I gazed about the hall and again marveled at the

meditators who were so ridiculously solemn. I felt as if a flippant, glib being had taken over my body and was trying to show me how everything was merely a dance. It was so liberating that the urge to laugh became uncontrollable. It was as if I was a child again at the dinner table with my father scolding me for giggling, and the more he scolded, the more I giggled.

I finally had to leave the hall before my laughter erupted, but when I went to my room and tried to relax, the giggling abruptly stopped.

During an unimaginable terror-filled night, wild random snippets of visions in vivid color raged through my mind with several flashing every second. The top half of my body was on fire and the bottom half ice cold with my heart pounding so severely that it would actually stop beating at times producing intense feelings of fear and impending death.

Then everything would suddenly stop, and my entire body would become numb. I could feel nothing; no heartbeat, no breathing, nothing. I had to move my fingers and toes to make sure that I was still alive. Every twenty minutes my body would alternate between these extremes, and during the night the symptoms worsened.

About four in the morning, I stumbled into the hallway for help. One of the retreat participants summoned the head monk, who in turn brought in a doctor that was fortunately attending the retreat, and after a cursory check of my heart, piled me into his car, and headed for San Francisco General Hospital.

The emergency room was packed. After waiting hours in agony, a nurse wheeled me into an examining room and hooked up an EKG. He took a quick look at the tape and said, "Hold on man, I'll get some help!"

For a moment, I was certain that I was dying, and was shocked when the intense fear disappeared, replaced by extreme peacefulness as if I was floating over the table. The feeling was so serene that to this day I cannot find words to describe it. I had experienced this kind of thing only once before, when I was eighteen and almost drowned in Lake Erie.

I was with some friends at the time and we all foolishly swam too far from shore hanging onto a large log. I was never a good swimmer, but as long as I had the log to hang onto, I was okay. A storm was coming up, however, and when the wind began pushing the log and us out into the lake, we left it behind and started swimming for shore. The shore, however, was a long way in, and I didn't think I could make it. I swam as far as I could but still was a long way from the beach. I tried to touch bottom and walk in, but there was no bottom to be found!

I fought back up to the surface but with the increasing turbulence and high waves, I soon became tired and again attempted to touch bottom. This time I went a long way under and barely made it to the surface again. Exhausted, I just couldn't swim any further and tried in desperation for the third time to touch bottom, knowing that if there was no bottom this time, I was finished. And there was no bottom.

I surrendered. I was dying. Then, the most profound peacefulness imaginable enveloped me like warm arms.

Suddenly the warm arms were grabbing my hair! One of men in the party, an excellent swimmer, saw me struggling and when he saw me go under and not come up, he swam down, grabbed me, and towed me to shore, where I promptly vomited for two hours. Everything changed that day, and this was my first memorable shift in consciousness.

I continued to lie peacefully on the gurney at San Francisco General until a physician arrived and quickly checked me out. He admitted that he had no idea what was going on and that only a battery of tests could possibly determine the problem. Janet and I were almost broke, as usual, with no insurance, so that was not an option.

Janet: "Ed returned to the Zen Center, and after a week the situation didn't improve. He could barely get around. The moment he tried to do anything, his heart would go crazy, his legs would go numb, and his blood pressure would soar. He tried to get into some free clinics in the Haight-Ashbury but he was too weak to remain in line for the hours it required. We were up against it again. With less than a thousand dollars in our pockets, we decided to head for Boulder – a place that was to become our refuge between journeys.

No matter where we found ourselves, an opportunity existed for discovery. Because adverse situations are defined as that opposed to what we want, they always forced us to learn something more about ourselves.

The Buddha said that wanting/desire is the root of human suffering. We were certainly learning about our suffering. Perhaps, however, no situation is adverse within the scope of the universe. I was slowly realizing that situations just 'are' on this road to enlightenment; a road that must be traveled as a limber tree gracefully bends with the wind, because stiff ones break.

We made our way to Boulder and set ourselves up in a small efficiency apartment. We had just enough money left over for some groceries. I was able to land a job with a home care agency, but without a car, I had to use busses to get around to the clients homes.

It was a difficult period for both of us. Ed was so sick and I was working so hard to keep things together. Ed could not stand up, nor even have simple conversations because everything was too intense, all magnified in some strange way. His heart would stop with the slightest exertion. He would have to crawl to the bathroom.

One day I surprised him with a present, a small houseplant that became his treasured friend. Because his strength was gone physically, emotionally and psychologically, all that he could do was lie in bed and watch the little plant in the corner grow – one leaf at a time."

Are life's disappointments connected to expectations? I dreamed about how it should be – and when it wasn't, my sense of fairness in some strange way seemed violated. What would it be like to have no expectations? Dull? Perhaps boring? Maybe I enjoyed my roller coaster trip of vicissitudes and subconsciously created them just for the ride. But what happens when the excitement stops? I was finding out.

9. Tangled Passageways

Janet was able to save enough money for some doctor's visits, but after three different doctors examined me, none could come up with a diagnosis. They had no idea what was wrong, and expensive tests were out of the question – I couldn't burden Janet with more bills. One of them at least prescribed a beta-blocker that helped, but it didn't help much.

I couldn't read or talk with anybody without my heart racing and palpitating wildly. The feeling of pressure in my chest was debilitating and my legs would go numb if I tried to walk. Any exertion, for example going to see a doctor, would insure nights of terror and sleeplessness. I had become extremely sensitive to everything, as if all my nerves were laid bare.

With no alternatives, I finally went to see a Tibetan monk and certified acupuncturist that Janet had heard about. After an examination, he said that I had somehow short-circuited subtle passageways in the body, and that this imbalance was impossible to diagnose or cure with conventional medicine.

After a few treatments, he admitted that it was the most stubborn case he had ever seen, caused by prematurely unleashing what he called the kundalini energy; a life force that sits at the base of the spine and moves upwards in spiritual release. He warned that whether I lived or died now depended entirely on how good my karma was from past lives, and how strong I was physically.

He consoled me by saying that not everything

about this illness was bad, that much of my past karma was being burned up so that if I lived, I could make great strides in my quest for enlightenment. It reminded me of something I read at the abbey; St. John of the Cross wrote that God will tear down a seeker's old body so that a new temple will be ready when God enters. I certainly felt torn down!

The monk suggested that I get a simple job out in nature for awhile, cutting wood or something, and counseled me that if I didn't stop meditating, I could kill myself – but I never stopped. I continued to practice from the day I became ill. If I died, I died. At least I would cash in my chips doing what I trusted most even if it was killing me.

My meditation was improving, but my health was not. Despite the Tibetan monk's valiant efforts of acupuncture treatments and cones of searing incense scarring my chest, no relief was in sight. With Janet burning out and things looking hopeless, I became frantic and contacted Trungpa Rinpoche's local Buddhist community, literally begging for help. Nobody there could come up with anything except for one person who told me about a chiropractor who was considered gifted.

A chiropractor? Gifted? But what other choice did I have. Maybe a back adjustment would help. I was desperate. A week later, I found myself lying on his table as he passed small vials of assorted substances over my chest while asking me to push on his hand so that he could detect any weaknesses. I couldn't believe this; I must have been really desperate to succumb to this quackery!

After the 'examination,' he sat me down in his office and prescribed 5,000 mg of vitamin C a day (vitamin C?) and warned me to stop eating all grains, especially wheat, for the rest of my life! There went the rice, spaghetti, and pizza! I could only eat meat, fish, poultry, eggs, dairy, fruits and vegetables. He claimed that something traumatic had occurred that created a sudden, severe allergy to grains, and that unless I stopped eating them, my condition would not improve.

Okay, Janet and I had already gambled a hundred bucks to see him, so why not a little more for some vitamin C and pork chops? What did I have to lose at this point?

Janet: "Initially, nothing much happened. After a few days, however, Ed thought that maybe, just maybe, there was some improvement, but he refused to believe it. He was far too skeptical of this 'doctor' and was sure that any improvement was only his imagination − a placebo effect.

A week later, however, he wasn't imagining things, not only was he vastly improved, but he could actually sleep and get around! This chiropractor was either gifted or lucky, and we didn't care which at this point; we were only happy that Ed was somewhat normal again."

I landed a part-time maintenance job with the apartment complex's property manager who befriended us and who wasn't the least bit concerned when I couldn't remain standing long enough for him to even show me how to fix a leaky faucet!

Over the years, I have experimented with grains many times only to find myself back in the same boat. When Zen sickness hits, it hits with a vengeance! If I could do it all over again, I probably would have taken time to cultivate a little compassion and love before going so deeply into concentration and focusing so hard with no relaxation. It's only jerks like me that get into trouble! Janet never had any problems at all.

I became resolved to the fact that I would never be as strong as I once was. St John of the Cross said it quite well – that when serious meditators make progress, many times they get sick as hell (that's a paraphrase). The grave mistake I made of forcing a crude mind to go deeply too quickly almost turned out to be lethal, but regardless of the illness, and perhaps because of it, my thirst for enlightenment mysteriously became stronger than ever.

I now understood, with my heart, that nothing of this world would ever satisfy me again. I was determined to find enlightenment no matter the cost and was willing to risk my life a hundred times over; my determination had become that powerful. What other choice did I have now?

One other unusual effect of the illness might be worth mentioning; my mind became amazingly sharp. I could analyze things in unbelievably minute detail where every aspect of a situation or problem would disclose itself immediately.

Because of the unseen benefits that this illness produced, I would have done everything all over again exactly the same way. Without this seemingly troublesome experience, I would have missed the opportunity to become reacquainted with my teacher – illness – a teacher who was stronger than my arrogance and forced me to discover much about myself, introducing me to so many selfless people who helped me through this ordeal.

The experience instilled an unshakeable resolve. No longer was there doubt about anything I was doing and I thirsted for another taste of that powerful transformation that hit me at the Zen Center, even though it dangerously compromised my health by nearly ended me.

The resolve was hard to explain, for it was not of this world, but I was enthralled. Now I understood those powerful, foolish sounding words when they appeared in San Francisco: "*You are now completely healed.*" I was healed, but not from illness; I was healed from falling prey to the delusions of the world. I was free at last to search for truth with all my heart, and although my body was seriously weakened, my resolve had now doubled.

Janet: "We didn't know if we would find truth quickly, slowly, or at all, but it was too late to go back to what we were before this search began. Stopping now would only wedge us between the world and enlightenment, a most unwelcome situation! We had to keep striving until striving was no longer necessary, and we would know when that happened.

With Ed's health improving, we worked a few years to get some cash together until it was time to get serious about our practice once more. A little signal would go off in our heads when it was time to move on. Was it restlessness or destiny?

Out in the middle of nowhere, near Tacoma, Washington is the little town of McKenna where a Zen Roshi from Shasta Abbey was in the beginning stages of establishing a monastery. To help him out, we rented a small house in the country and spent our days in a green, lush forest digging holes to gauge for soil absorption, clearing land and getting ready to build.

In the evenings, we meditated with the Roshi, and to make ends meet, I again worked at a homecare agency while Ed worked in a gas station and did odd jobs out of an old Toyota pickup truck in nearby Yelm, WA. But this was just a respite, a quick stopover before we again went overseas."

After escaping from rainy Washington State, we dived right into rainy UK, with our new destination Amaravati, a Buddhist monastery located forty kilometers north of London. It sat on rural agricultural land surrounded by farm fields and blossoming fruit trees that thrived beautifully in the relentless showers.

My job was to help cut the twenty acres of perpetually soggy grass and help drive people back and forth to London — on the wrong side of the road for this yank! The endless roundabouts were only outdone by the narrow, curvy hedgerows that were really one-lane sixty kilometers per hour green tunnels where people tried to drive two-ways. That was interesting because although there was not enough room to pass each other, except for an occasional wide spot in the road, the Brits had ESP and knew if something was coming around the next curve. Yanks not so much!

Particularly memorable at Amaravati were the bi-monthly all-night meditation sessions, reminiscent of Thailand, and the hot tea, coffee and chocolates that were passed around at midnight to keep us going. Amaravati enabled us to go deeper, and the deeper we went the more there was to discover because even though we saw things we had always seen before, we were seeing them with wider eyes. Everything was a new adventure. How incredibly unfathomable was this practice of meditation.

Janet: "Before ordaining as anagarikas at Amaravati, we buried our wedding rings in a new stupa (a dome-shaped Buddhist shrine) that was being built. This was symbolic in moving from a personal relationship to an expanded relationship within the principles of Buddhism, and in our case, specifically Buddhist meditation. During my time there as an anagarika, I grew fond of Amaravati and eventually found my way back."

Before long, the snowy mountains of Boulder, our old stomping grounds, beckoned us to return for a breather. I could now tell almost immediately whether or not a geographical area was conducive to my meditation, and Boulder was. Janet thrived in the UK with the wonderful group of nuns there, but for me, the UK didn't work, and although Janet loved the community, she reluctantly returned with me to Boulder.

We found it difficult to push or hurry things along as we had in the past, once we were back in Boulder. All that we wanted to do at this point was sit and wait, surrendering to that which was growing in our hearts. We bought an old ten by forty-eight foot house trailer for $1,600 in Boulder, reconditioned it, and practiced on our own for six years.

Janet: "I worked in a three-hundred bed nursing home, both in the assisted living section as well as its Alzheimer's ward, while Ed started a one-man plumbing and electrical repair business. We didn't join any groups, but occasionally stayed in snow-covered cab-

ins at the Tibetan Buddhist's Shambhala Mountain Center in Red Feather, CO.

Boulder was always a cultural panacea that was spiritually alive, and one day we noticed a flyer tacked to a utility pole on the Boulder pedestrian mall advertising a two-day intensive meditation retreat in the neighboring town of Broomfield. Since we had never attended a retreat hosted by a Korean Zen master before, we decided to go.

The retreat was held in a large home on a pretty piece of property surrounded by beautiful trees and flowers, a nice setting, and we were surprised how many people decided to attend. I wasn't aware at the time that the Korean Zen master was considered to be enlightened, and known worldwide!"

After we were all seated and facing the various walls, the schedule and rules were covered, and then we began to meditate. I was happily meditating on the second day when I felt a tap on my shoulder.

"Would you like an interview with the Zen master?"

"Sure," I whispered, thinking, '*Why not? I don't need any help, but who knows, he might have something interesting to say.*'

I was taken upstairs to the rear of the house where I found him sitting on a meditation cushion in the middle of a huge room. He was holding a weird staff that looked like a crooked tree limb growing out of the floor, and a funny hat that looked quite comical, although he wasn't smiling. I entered the room, bowed respectfully, and then just stood there for a moment not knowing what to do. He pointed to the cushion across from him, indicating that I should sit, after which I sat quietly for a moment until he loudly announced, "WHERE YOU COME FROM?"

Wow! Where do I come from? This was undoubtedly a metaphysical question with which he was testing me, and while I was thinking about where I fundamentally came from, or even who "I" was, he banged his staff on the floor impatiently and repeated, "WHERE YOU COME FROM?"

I thought to myself, *Slow down Zen master, I'm thinking, I'm thinking, Hmm . . . I am just an emanation of the Fundamental Reality . . . no that's not quite right. Maybe I . . .*

BANG, there went the staff again as he shouted, "DON'T KNOW!"

I looked at him, puzzled, and he banged the stick again, "DON'T KNOW! DON'T KNOW!" he yelled.

I finally got the idea and repeated, "DON'T KNOW?"

"Good," he said, "now . . . what are you?"

Whoa, another great, deep question! And as I tried to figure this one out, there went the staff . . . BANG! "DON'T KNOW, DON'T KNOW . . . STUPID!" he yelled again.

Sheepishly, I repeated, "DON'T KNOW!"

"Good," he said, and then went on to ask more questions, but now I had the hang of it and every time he asked a question, I quickly replied, "DON'T KNOW!"

As he asked more questions, I became very confident with my "DON'T KNOWS" answering almost before he finished his question. My replies were becoming very animated! "DON'T KNOW! DON'T KNOW! DON'T KNOW!" This was fun.

Then he asked, "What's your name?" and of

course, I replied, smiling, "DON'T KNOW!"

He looked at me quizzically, smiled thinly, raised his eyebrows and said, "You don't know your own name?"

Something suddenly hit me. I don't know what or why, but something changed deep inside right then and there – a definite shift in consciousness brought about by a little man in a funny hat that absolutely blew my arrogant mind away.

He pointed to the door and I knew my interview was over, an interview only a few minutes long but one that I would never forget.

The retreat was one of the best two days I had ever spent, and when I left the hall that afternoon, the trees and flowers surrounding the property were different; they were dazzling, and they have dazzled ever since.

It was already 1993 and Janet, as saintly as she was, was not Supergirl and eventually burned herself out trying to help her nursing home patients. This was compounded by feelings of inadequacy and competition from the other aides who were studying to become nurses, while Janet was satisfied to just practice meditation and remain an aide.

Janet: "One night I told Ed that I could no longer continue at the nursing home. Knowing that it wouldn't be long before Ed's parents, who were having health problems, would need Ed, their only child, to help out in Pennsylvania, we weren't sure what to do. Ed was OK with handling that himself, and just wanted me to be content and follow my heart. He asked me what it was that I really wanted to do.

Holding back tears, I told him that I wanted to return to Amaravati and live again as a nun, and then I really began crying, knowing that this would not only involve our being separated for possibly years, but that I would not be beside him to help with his parents."

Neither of us ever forgot our vow to help each other find truth in this lifetime, and this was how I could help her now. I was going to give her time to train by herself rather than dragging her along to Pennsylvania for what could be a long ordeal.

Janet: "Although I felt guilty leaving my nursing home patients, I had to go with my heart. Someday, I hoped to be an example for somebody, and even if that somebody was only one person who might begin their own quest for enlightenment, I would be satisfied. I longed to return to the company of those who understood my feelings. Working in the nursing home and keeping my understanding to myself was a most difficult thing."

That night, after we had made our decision, we held each other for a long time and later, when I was meditating in my bedroom, a voice in my mind said, *"The only difference between life and death is the breath."* I didn't yet know what that meant.

Chapter Ten

10. The Forest Never Noticed

While Janet was living in the UK, I was writing and distributing free meditation booklets around Boulder. I offered classes at our little trailer but hardly anybody showed up. People would drive by and look in occasionally, but the trailer park was small, and our trailer, although newly painted, was tiny and old. It was the best that I could do at the time.

I eventually sold the trailer and gave all of our stuff away, again, thinking about the number of times we had accumulated stuff only to give it all away. I made my way to Pennsylvania on a Greyhound carrying all my worldly belongings in a backpack – my preferred way to travel.

Janet: "Ed's mother was suffering from Alzheimer's and in a nursing home thirty miles upstate from his father's government assisted one room apartment. It wasn't easy for his father to get back and forth on the bus to see her, but he still made the trip religiously three times a week even though he had little money and was just getting by. Nothing seems to last – the poor man runs out of money, the rich man runs out of life."

My father moved around a lot during his time on this earth. He was always happier in a different place and wasn't much for settling down. He liked new things to do and new people to meet, but got bored with it all pretty fast, too. Something would happen to discourage him, and he would be off again thinking that a different town would be the answer, or sometimes he would spend a few years in his hometown in Pennsylvania to regroup. He always looked forward to hitting the road, even hopping freight cars and riding the rails down to Florida and back.

One time he settled down, long enough to build a house by himself out in the Ohio farm country. We lived there until I was eighteen, when I headed for Furman University with my high school sweetheart and new wife, and I never came back. He sold the house soon afterward.

He was now fed up with living in the subsidized, state funded housing development; he was tired of everything, but it was too late, his options had run out. A new place would be fine again, for awhile, but now as he looked in a mirror that reflected an old man that time had passed by, he was becoming frightened. The money had run out and there were no more moves to make. All he had left was a wife in a nursing home and a son who was just like him in so many ways. My heart went out to him because I was no different, trying to find contentment in a world steeped in discontent.

While some men move on, others stay put. We are all enslaved in one way or the other, until one day we wake up and we are old, and all the amusements that we counted on so desperately become stale as well.

My dad was down to earth and had courage in many ways, but now, what he had been looking for his entire life was not to be found, and he didn't know where to turn. He was tired, and was left with just loneliness.

Loneliness terrified him; it covered him like a blanket. His wife had truly been a quiet saint all her life, and now that her mind was gone, she was destined to die in an Alzheimer's ward with my father trying to make up for things in his own way.

The rest of Dad's time would go quickly, and when he did die, I was certain that he would find himself more attached to this transient world than inclined to give it up and go on. I could have talked to him about all of this, but I didn't. It wouldn't have changed things. Until he could feel the pain of this worldly existence in his heart, he wouldn't listen. The only way he would know about these things is when he relaxed from his desperate escapes – something he and I were yet to understand.

One evening my father went to his closet, emerged with two wrinkled old coats and laid them on the table. Small bills, tens and twenties, were sewn in the linings that he had apparently been saving for years. The next day he put this life's savings in a paper sack and asked me to accompany him to the local funeral parlor. He spread the crumpled money on a desk, looked at the director, and asked, "Is this enough?"

The funeral director counted the three thousand dollars that was lying there and nodded, assuring my dad that everything would be taken care of. Mom and dad would be buried together in a small cemetery in the Pennsylvania foothills. I had a little money that would have helped, but this act of finality was important to him, something he had to do himself. Perhaps in his mind it was a closure that made amends for his checkered past. When one's lifetime partner dies, neither the saint nor sinner's regrets are far apart.

I was torn. Should I stay with him or continue my

search for enlightenment, something that, of course, was nowhere but right here with my father who needed help. Yet I was far from realizing that. With Janet practicing hard at Amaravati and remaining true to our vow, would she be better off if we now went our separate ways without me bothering her with my restless meanderings.

I sat with the decision for some time, with that silent voice inside nagging me to support Janet. I couldn't go to the UK; that would be too disruptive for her as well as the good people at the monastery because I would probably end up leaving and make a mess of things again.

Janet: "This is the second time that I stayed at Amaravati, but this time it was by myself while Ed was dealing with his parents in Pennsylvania. For the first year, our separation was very difficult for me and I missed Ed a lot. It made me realize how hard it will be if he dies first, but with meditation, along with time, I found myself adapting to his absence making the second year easier.

I was very fond of Amaravati, especially the twice a month all night sittings where we meditated until dawn. I also had many interesting encounters. One that stands out was when in desperation I visited a healer. I really didn't believe in healers, but a nun told me about one that helped her, so I thought what the heck, I'll try it.

Surprise, surprise! After having to take two different busses to get to his place, not only did he cure my ailment but also he said that I was capable of healing people long distance.

The men and women in white (anagarikas) who

were training eventually to ordain as monks and nuns took turns as the head cook of the monastery for three months at a time. For me, this was very challenging because I never learned to cook, especially for more than twenty or thirty people every day! Luckily, however, other anagarikas and lay people helped out, plus, being the head cook meant that you had no other duties after lunch.

When I wasn't cooking, I would do some chores in the mornings and afternoons for a total of about four hours; for example cleaning, vacuuming, kitchen help, weeding, raking, and general maintenance. I especially liked doing outside work.

One day we had a surprise visit from a female nun who had just been in India practicing for ten years. This was a stopover for her before moving on to Australia with the intention of eventually establishing a nun's monastery.

For some reason we made an immediate connection and she asked me if I would like to go to Australia with her to help start a place for nuns to ordain on some land that was already available to her. It was a huge decision for me. I wanted to go with her, but something inside said to stay at Amaravati. Years later I heard that she was ordained by Ajahn Brahm as a bhikkhuni – a full Buddhist nun equal to a Buddhist monk."

Just as I was pondering what to do regarding supporting Janet or staying with my father, karma intervened, as it often does. It was a letter from Janet, and the letter was short. Janet's oldest sister was dying.

Janet: "When I received news of my sister dying, I

was undecided about what to do. But in the end, my sister was near death and I wanted to be with her when she died."

Janet left the UK on her way to her sister's house in Tionesta that was coincidentally only a few hours north of where I was staying with my dad. When I told Dad that I would be gone for awhile to help Janet with her sister, he became jealous, even though I assured him that it wouldn't be for long.

The day before I left, almost as if rebelling against my leaving, he tripped in the apartment and hit his arm on the table as he fell, tearing a swatch of his paper thin skin from the inside of his forearm. "The hell with it," he said, while smoothing the skin back onto his arm and wrapping it with a Walmart bag and scotch tape. He was always the tough guy in many ways, but in many ways, he was so vulnerable, as we all are.

The bus ride up to Tionesta brought back a flood of memories from the oil drilling days, and I couldn't wait to see my partner again. It had been a couple of years. She couldn't wait either to tell me about her uncanny experience with a healer and her day-to-day challenges and achievements at Amaravati. She was still ordained, wearing her white skirt and blouse and sporting a bald head, but she always looked beautiful to me. Janet had the kindest heart that I had ever run across, and she was unswervingly dedicated to our vow. My heart went out to her once again.

Her sister was a genuinely good person, quiet and unassuming. I never heard her say one unkind word about anybody. But she had been a heavy smoker and was now diagnosed with incurable lung cancer. The

Cleveland Clinic only gave her six months to live, and five had gone by.

We stayed with Janet's relatives and occasionally some Hospice people at her sister's picturesque cabin on the Allegheny River where we all took turns caring for her. Janet's sister was so happy to see Janet and Janet's bald head because now Janet's sister no longer felt she had to cover up her baldness from the Chemo.

But she was suffering one lung infection after another and in and out of the hospital, and one afternoon a doctor took her husband aside and told him that she had only weeks to live, possibly days.

We brought her back to the cabin and in the wee hours of the morning on the day that she died, there were a series of strange occurrences that were extraordinarily and bizarre. I wrote them down afterward and discussed them with Janet and her sister's husband to make sure that they witnessed the same things that I did, and they both agreed.

Janet was taking a turn sitting with her sister while I was asleep in an adjoining room. It was about two in the morning when, half awake, I heard Janet running down the hall. She burst into the room whispering frantically, "She can't breathe, she can't breathe!" I glanced at the wall separating our room from her sister's and saw what appeared to be heat waves rising on the wall. I thought, 'That's strange, it's summertime,' and when I put my hand on the heater as I hurried out . . . it was dead cold.

Janet: "My sister was trying to sit up, clawing at her mask. She was receiving large volumes of oxygen from tanks behind her bed, both through a mask and a nose tube. They surgically embedded a small dispens-

151

ing device in her side to release a constant flow of morphine, but the pain was unrelenting and we had to inject additional doses into her thigh every hour as well. I tried to hold her in a sitting position but she was fighting and hysterical. It was very emotional for me.

Then, suddenly, her breathing stopped and she went limp. We carefully laid her back on the bed, watching for her breathing to resume – no heroic measures at this point – but it didn't. She just lay there, unmoving, and it became apparent she wasn't coming back. We tried to detect a breath, but nothing, only the humming of the oxygen generators. Ed looked at me and shook his head. I was crying as I left the room to awaken my brother-in-law.

He was understandably distraught, with the burden of my sister's horrible suffering over the last many months taking its toll. Very tenderly, he removed the oxygen mask and nose tube. Sobbing, he took her limp body into his arms and said, "I loved you, Baby, I loved you so much."

"I love you too," she replied.

We all jumped back as if we'd seen a ghost. There she was, with no oxygen, calmly looking at us with a radical change in her demeanor. She was peaceful, strong, and her voice was different – deeper and measured. This was no longer my sister.

She had made a pact with her husband in the past that the first one to go would somehow come back and communicate with the other. Her husband must have felt this was happening now because he asked her, incredulously, "What's it like?"

Smiling, she said, "There were beautiful people, and beautiful music."

Then, apparently wanting to let her know that it was okay for her to let go, end her suffering and leave this earth, and also that she had fulfilled her promise to come back and communicate after death, he said, "It's okay, Baby; you can go on now, you don't have to stay here. I'll be there with you soon."

Then she said something that stunned all of us, especially her husband. Looking unblinkingly into his eyes, she calmly and quietly said, "You can't come where I have been."

This unnerving, confident declaration sent chills up and down all of our spines. This was not the meek-mannered woman we had come to know; the quiet unassuming soul who was so humble and self-effacing that she would never think of talking this outspokenly to anybody, let alone her husband.

"What!" He sputtered. "What do you mean, 'I can't come there?'"

Looking at him as a kind teacher would look at a favorite student who was failing, she said, "No, you have to be good, and you have to be on the path."

This is where I thought I might have misheard her. She had been a devout Roman Catholic all her life and the term 'path' was just not in the vernacular. The word 'path,' however, was confirmed by both Ed and her husband later that day when we all sat down and compared what we just witnessed.

After that, she quietly talked to her only child, her son, who later said that she asked him to get properly married in a church (which he and his wife eventually did). It was as if she was offering her loved ones advice that could alter their destinies, destinies she might have been able to foresee. This was all occurring with no oxygen being administered at all. Shortly *after speaking with her son, relatives gathered and prayed by her bedside until she went into a coma-like sleep, not long after which she stopped breathing for good.*

Words on paper can't begin to describe the eerie feelings we felt. Every hair on our bodies stood on end during the entire episode. We could not believe what we were witnessing. Ed seeing waves on the wall were unusual enough, but then to see my sister change personalities and say with such certainty that her husband could not follow her to wherever it was that she went, was beyond comprehension, and definitely proof that I didn't know anything about this incredible universe.

The monks in Thailand talked about ghosts and spirits as if they were common place, but this was the first time that I had ever experienced anything first hand. This episode with my sister increased my faith in everything the monks had told us about rebirth and past lives, leaving no doubt that the path we were on was the correct one for us."

After a quiet funeral, Janet accompanied me to Johnstown to meet my parents for the first time. She was still in white robes with a shaved head, and Dad, still jealous of me taking the time to help Janet with her sister, insulted her bald head and the way she was dressed. Janet didn't become angry or try to defend herself; she only cried. She understood that he was frightened. For me, I understood something, too.

When Janet and I bussed out to the nursing home to visit my mother, she was still able to recognize me but wondered who Janet was. I believe she thought Janet was a bald nurse in a white uniform! It was a nice visit; both women had a unique, unspoken quality in their hearts that they recognized in each other.

Soon, I was putting Janet on a bus to the Pittsburgh airport where she would head back to the UK and Amaravati monastery. Amaravati had established a branch monastery in New Zealand, and it was there that I decided to go. It would be a perfect place to train because I could both support Janet by joining the same group as hers, as well as being half way around the world and too far away to disturb her training.

I had already made my decision to leave Pennsylvania when Dad mistreated and insulted Janet, the kindest person I had ever known, so badly that it made her cry.

He tried to control my mother and me our entire lives, and now that was going to stop. I understood that he was merely frightened and jealous of my attention, but I was also rudely reminded of the unkindness he had shown to my mother – his drunkenness, carousing, and disrespect.

All of us are guilty sooner or later of abusing others in some way, but I felt I had no choice if I was to stay true to our vow. Still, although the decision was spontaneous, it was not easy, but in the end my overriding concern became Janet, and I would take care of her the best way that I could.

The day I left, I glanced up from the parking lot and saw my father looking out the window. Neither of us waived goodbye.

Before I left for the Southern Hemisphere, I needed a place to deprogram for awhile. I wanted to get back on track with my meditation as well as make arrangements for my trip to New Zealand, and the best place to do that was not far away.

The Bhavana Society means "mental development" in Pali. It is tucked away in the hills of the picturesque state of West Virginia, and just down the road from Johnstown. Bhante G, a Sri Lankan monk and world recognized meditation teacher, welcomed me to the monastery and retreat center in the same warm manner that all serious seekers are welcomed in Theravada Buddhist organizations. They never charge fees and only ask that the seeker meditates seriously and helps out the community in whatever capacity he or she can.

The time at Bhavana went by quickly. I kept busy with paperwork preparing to travel oversees as well as felling trees, splitting firewood, working in the kitchen and later pitching in with the construction of the new meditation hall. It was peaceful, waking up every morning at 5 a.m. to the big 'gong' and then meditating for an hour and a half before starting our day. I even had my own little cabin with a woodstove! My mind calmed down quickly at Bhavana, and I would have remained there with Bhante G and ordained as one of his monks, but I wanted to support Janet by becoming part of Amaravati.

One pretty fall day, just as the trees were beginning to display their red and orange magnificence, Bhante G came over to where I was helping lay blocks for the foundation of the meditation hall. We chatted for awhile, and after he returned to his office, a nun came running out waving an email in her hand. My travel and visa arrangements had been approved.

When I first arrived, I donated a few copies of some of my meditation pamphlets to the Bhavana library. One of them was a story that must have struck a chord because I overheard a monk reading it to a gathering of visitors the day before I left. It was the story of a little tree . . .

. . . that had a special place all to itself in a beautiful forest, and with the warm winds and gentle rains, the seedling began to grow. Soon, a few small leaves appeared and the little tree spent the long summer days opening itself to the sun.

For some reason, however, growing straight and tall in this wonderful sunny spot was not enough, something was missing; the little seedling was lonely and needed friends. Before long, other little trees gathered round and the little tree was finally happy.

The other trees began to grow tall and sturdy, but the poor little seedling, now covered by their shade, could hardly grow at all. This didn't matter, however, because the little tree's only concern was the happiness of its friends.

Winters came, followed by springs, and time stood still — yet time somehow moved as the little tree, just a few feet tall, found itself surrounded by giant trees. They were so tall that the little tree could barely see their tops, and sadly, it lost touch with them, but was happy nonetheless now that its friends had grown so big and strong.

Years later, one of the large trees, now old and diseased, fell over and crushed the little tree. The little tree's heart was broken, not because it now lay under a huge, dead log, but because its old friend had died and would no longer feel the wind through its branches and the sun on its leaves — things the little tree could remember from long ago. And in thinking about its friend, the little tree forgot all about itself.

Only one of its tiny leaves could be seen peeking out from under the massive log that had fallen on it, but as the old tree fell, it also opened a window in the canopy of the forest. For the first time since it was a small seedling, the little tree felt the warmth of the sun as it touched its solitary leaf.

The years continued to pass, as they do, and another tree fell, then another until the little tree was alone again. In time, it was able to grow out from under its fallen friend and although it was now twisted and deformed from its efforts, it blamed nobody and was at peace with itself and the forest.

The little tree could never see beyond its small, special home in the wilderness, but somehow it became very wise. It knew joy — of the sun and of the wind, and it learned how to accept darkness as well. It understood that things sometimes happen beyond our control, and, more importantly, that love can only happen beyond our control.

It could see that small trees sometimes are criticized by not living up to their potential of becoming large trees, and how, sadly, they might then try very hard to become something they can never be, not seeing the beauty of what they already are.

It believed that within the insignificance of little trees could be found the greatness of large trees, but whether they were great or small, the little tree loved them all.

It never grew very big, living out its life reaching toward the light, and then, one beautiful spring morning it died — so quietly and peacefully that

. . . the forest never even noticed.

New Zealand was stunning, once I got there on the twenty-six hour flight that went on forever. About eighteen hours out, we hit a cloudbank that continued all the way to Auckland, a phenomenon that I was later to discover was stationary, more or less, over the rain soaked islands.

The four-hundred kilometer train trip from tropical Auckland to the rainforests of Wellington was breathtaking. I could honestly say that every bend in the tracks was a picture postcard — from mountains, to ocean, to pastoral pastures of grazing sheep. The locals would tell you that if you straighten out all the wrinkles in New Zealand it would be the size of Australia! That's a *stretch,* but the country really does have few flatlands, with the South Island, even sporting Colorado inspired snowcapped mountains. The homes and streets in Wellington were no different from middle class neighborhoods in Des Moines, very Americanized but with no street signs. When I inquired about this apparent oversight, I was told that I should know where I'm going . . . hmm.

The monastery grounds were nestled among a series of great folds in the earth covered with rainforest foliage, and it was on one of these hills that I hung my hat. The small cabin was half way up the mountain and very upscale compared to the kutis that I was accustomed to in Thailand. It even had a sliding glass door and porch where possums loved to sit and watch me in the evenings while I meditated with my candle.

Possums populated the southern island like a blanket because somebody introduced them years ago forgetting that there are no natural predators to control them! But they became my friends; I always seemed to attract friendly animals no matter where I found myself.

The cabin was difficult to find during the day, let alone at night when I had to climb the mountain in the dark and rain to retire. A couple of steps off the path without a flashlight and you'd be finished, so I always kept spare batteries in my pocket, just in case.

The Wellington weather was wetter than Washington State or the UK. The rain was intense, unremitting, and came down sideways many times making my nocturnal trek from the meditation hall up the mountainside to my cabin challenging, to say the least.

Then one night it happened – halfway up my flashlight went out. I fumbled in my pocket for the spare batteries muttering, "Thank goodness, thank goodness," but when I switched them with the old ones . . . no light. It was the bulb, and I didn't have a spare. I couldn't make out a thing in the driving rain and ink-black forest; I couldn't even see my hand in front of my face, so I was left with two alternatives, both bad – either hunker down where I was for a cold and wet night, or feel my way through the forest.

Toughing it out in the storm all night wasn't an appealing prospect, and since I had a general idea of the path's direction, I decided to try to make it to my cabin. Fortunately, there are no perilous creatures in New Zealand, no poisonous snakes or dangerous animals, so my only concern was staying on the path and not being loved to death by possums!

I stooped down and could actually feel the edge of the trail, encouraging me to continue on my hands and knees as I started crawling home. Feeling around in the mud and rain wasn't pleasant, and many times, I wasn't even sure that I was still on the trail, but about an hour later, I finally felt the front porch of my cabin. I slithered in, wrapped up in a blanket and lit a candle, and started a cup of tea on my Sterno burner. When I glanced out at the porch, a trio of possums was lined up along my sliding glass door laughing at me, or so it appeared. They had no problem at all getting around in the black forest on a stormy night.

One evening I was staring at the Southern Cross, that beautiful constellation we can't see in the Northern hemisphere, when I found myself reflecting on these monks in New Zealand, as well as all the people I had met who were involved in this strange pursuit of enlightenment. I couldn't help but feel a strong tug in my heart for these folks living just that small step above oblivion, and for the immensity of a practice, that was such a life changer.

One day I tried to reach my father for the first time since I left West Virginia, but the phone was disconnected. He had no friends or relatives to speak of, so I began calling local hospitals, one of which informed me that he was in a nursing home due to kidney failure and was getting dialysis treatments. Although I had written him with my phone number in New Zealand, he never called or wrote back, but that's how he was.

I booked a flight to Pittsburgh and bussed up to Johnstown where I talked my way into some public housing in the same building where Dad had lived – a room on the seventh floor without air conditioning. I was accustomed to heat after living in Thailand, so it was fine, and it was only two miles from Dad's nursing home, an easy walk to visit him after work every day.

Janet: "I wanted to return to the States and help Ed, but he talked me out of it. He wanted me to remain in England and continue my training, being true to our vow. He said that he could handle things in Pennsylvania for now."

I went through a flurry of jobs and finally saved enough money to buy an old Toyota for $600. The car was a big help because now I could drive over to see Mom once a week instead of spending an entire day working around bus schedules. My mother was going downhill fast.

Before I left for New Zealand she still recognized people and had a semblance of long-term memory, but now that was all gone. She didn't know me at all when I visited, and only stared ahead into space as if she was in a waking coma. I would talk to her, telling her about dad and the little stories that a son tells his mother, but there were never signs of awareness. She could still feed herself when the nurse brought her tray, but stared straight into the wall the entire time and only occasionally talking to the little flowers that bordered the ceiling.

I would wheel her outside on nice days, but that didn't matter, the unrelenting unawareness remained. She had gone through the anger stage a few years prior, but it was not very pronounced and thankfully short lived.

She always had a kind heart, and during her life exhibited only humility and humbleness, always worrying about everybody but herself. It was hard to see her like this, but she became one of my greatest teachers, reminding me to reach for enlightenment while my mind was still functioning. When it's gone, the search is over for this lifetime. Fortunately, my meditation had already shown me that my mind was merely transient, as were all my senses – nothing about which to get excited.

One day when I was visiting my father, he asked me to shave him and take him for a ride to his old neighborhood. It wasn't too far away. He was quiet during the trip, and it was shortly thereafter that he died.

The dialysis treatments that were keeping him alive took its inevitable toll on his heart and lungs, and one day his doctor took me aside and said that the treatments were no longer a viable option, meaning that he would die within a week.

Chapter Eleven

11. A Handful of Dirt

My father loved seeing me when I visited him at the nursing home. He would always be sitting in his wheelchair at the entrance to the home waiting for me to arrive. My visits were all he had to look forward to now, and he always wanted to hear any news about Mom. It was difficult to watch him die.

I vowed to hold both my parents' hands when they drew their last breath, and as things turned out, it was one of the best decisions I had ever made. It was something that's done with no thought of personal advantage, just something that would help another human being feel that he or she was not alone when his or her time came.

It was Halloween eve and Dad was in his last hours. He was still conscious but having difficulty breathing. The nurses were dressed up in cute costumes, coming around with little baskets of candy in a holiday mood – a marked contrast to the situation Dad was facing. I didn't say anything; this was not their problem.

I had gotten to know the three roommates sharing Dad's hospital room quite well, but this evening, I had the curtains drawn around Dad's bed. They had grown fond of him during the time he was there, and they understood that they would soon be facing what he was facing that night.

I sat beside my father and held his frail, bony hand, so old and veined with bruised, pasty skin as thin as paper. Surely, I thought, my strong body would never come to this.

Death was immanent; all he could manage were shallow gasps as his breathing was now sporadic with intervals where he didn't breathe at all. This went on for quite awhile and I was surprised when he suddenly sat up in bed and cried out, "We have to get out of here!" He surely saw something that frightened him badly. Then he laid back down, and after a few minutes, whispered, "I wish I would have done a few more good things in my life." I was shocked.

That was the last thing he said, and with his lungs filling with fluid he soon drew his last breath. I then watched an artery beat in his neck for over a minute until it, as well, became still. The words I heard in meditation in Boulder now came back to me, *"The only difference between life and death is the breath."*

I walked to the nurse's station where they were laughing and having a great time with the residents, and I didn't see any reason to bother them; after all, what was the hurry? I waited until one of the nurses acknowledged me and then told her that my dad had passed away. She brushed it off, saying that he will go through periods of feigning death well before he actually dies, but added that when she had time, she'd stop by.

About ten minutes later, she came in and checked his vitals. She was surprised to find him deceased, but remained business-like as she matter-of-factly asked me to leave for a few minutes while she prepared him for transport to the funeral home.

I looked for something to put his stuff in, finally borrowing a small garbage bag from an aide. I was pretty emotional as I put dad's few things in the bag, just some outdated checkered slacks, and a few faded shirts with worn collars. One of Dad's roommates was lying in the bed next to the closet. He wouldn't look at me; maybe he was embarrassed. He was laying on his side and appeared to be sleeping, but a telltale tear ran down his cheek. I don't think he had any family; at least nobody ever came to visit him, and I couldn't think of anything to say. I just touched his shoulder and walked away.

Only the undertaker along with two graveyard workers and a backhoe were at the small cemetery in the foothills where Dad was laid to rest. Nobody was there to say good-bye except me, and I wasn't sure what to do. As the workers lowered the casket, I took a handful of dirt and threw it on the coffin. I don't know why; maybe I saw it in a movie or something.

And that was my dad's life.

I recalled a monk in Thailand telling me about old age and death. He said that no one could escape it unless they become enlightened, and that until we truly understand, we would travel in a circle of birth, old age, disease, and death forever where our tears would fill the seas.

My tears that day simply evaporated I guess, but perhaps they would make it back to their source somehow, those mighty oceans. As I left the graveyard, I glanced back at the hole in the ground and wished my dad good luck in whatever situation his karma had in store for him. Spiritual seeds were sprouting from tiny cracks in the hard pavement of my controlled existence. It was those little interruptions – the accident, the illness, perhaps a death – that opened doors for me. Why couldn't I step through?

During the drive to Mom's nursing home, I found

myself torn. Should I tell her of Dad's passing or not? She probably wouldn't understand, but I couldn't be sure of that. Who knows what goes on in the minds of people in her condition? If by chance she did understand, the news would be devastating and take just about everything away that she had left. She loved him; I could always see it in her eyes.

I asked her nurse, who had been taking care of her for years, what she thought about the situation. She replied that it wouldn't hurt to tell her because she wouldn't understand anyway. When the nurse and I walked in to see Mom, she was sitting there as usual, but this time she wasn't staring at the wall – she was staring directly at me! Her dark, brown eyes pierced my very soul as she slowly raised her hand to her forehead and made the sign of the cross.

Both the nurse and I stopped dead in our tracks; something supernatural was taking place. She knew that Dad was gone.

I stared at her in disbelief, and just that quickly she looked away as if nothing had happened, falling back into her self-enclosed world.

I asked the nurse if she had ever seen anything like that before in the Alzheimer's ward, to which she indicated 'no' by shaking her head and raising her eyebrows as if she couldn't believe it either. I sat by Mom's side and went through the motions of telling her about Dad's final moments, how he died, and his last words, but she showed no interest or recognition whatsoever. When the nurse brought in her tray, she ate as if I wasn't there. She didn't live too long after this.

Janet: "I left the UK to join Ed (over Ed's pro-

tests) and we eventually moved from Johnstown to Winchester, Virginia, hoping for a better chance for employment even though none of these small Appalachian towns could offer much. Winchester was only an hour's drive from the Bhavana Society and Bhante 'G.' It was just over the line in West Virginia and a couple of hours from Ed's mother's nursing home in Pennsylvania, so we were able to deepen our practice and at the same time keep an eye on his mother."

We convinced a property manager in Winchester to take a chance on us in the way of a small apartment, which wasn't easy with our spotty history, Janet's nearly bald head, and the old, rusty Toyota that mystically kept running. It's strange how whenever we didn't have or want much, our karma was kind to us.

We cruised some garage sales and thrift stores in order to get a few things together like a phone to keep in touch with the nursing home. Luckily, we were accustomed to sleeping on bare, wooden floors in Thailand, so sleeping on a carpeted floor was a luxury. Whenever we found ourselves separated from monasteries, day jobs were required to pay the bills. Nobody was there to back us up.

Although our practice was now stable regardless of our involvements, our hearts yearned to do something connected to meditation rather than devoting all our time and energy to day jobs. But I couldn't leave Mom here in Pennsylvania to make it on her own. I made a promise to hold her hand when she died, and I had to stay close.

Janet tried selling furniture at a couple of different stores while I found myself going through four jobs in

169

only a short while. The minute I perceived unfairness or underhandedness of any kind by an employer, I would quit on the spot. Although I never had an appetite for appeasement, I did have a knack of selling myself, so landing a job was never a problem.

Janet: "We would make the trip from Virginia to Pennsylvania a couple of times a week to visit Ed's mom. It was a beautiful drive through the backcountry roads of Amish country. Ed's mom never changed, however, she never recognized him except for that one time after Ed's dad died. One day the nursing home called and said that nothing more could be done with her congestive heart failure. She didn't have long to live.

She was in a private room, which was very kind, and we took turns sitting with her and then sleeping in the chapel. One night I came into the chapel and put my hand on Ed's shoulder. I knew it was her time."

Her eyes were closed and her breathing was labored. I felt so helpless. My heart went out to my mother who so loved her little house in Ohio and the fields her only son played in, but she couldn't remember that anymore.

I drifted back to what a monk had told me about attachment and wanting, and how those two things are the root of our discontent. Right now, I had to admit that painful feelings were coming up as I recalled how hard she worked at dead-end jobs her entire life, sacrificing the little things she would have liked to have just to please my father and me.

One day when I was little, we went to a circus that was in town and my dad bought her an inexpensive pin at one of the booths. She loved that little cheap pin and wore it all the time; it was from the man she would always love. How could I not feel touched by her life; an expression of complete love by a faithful friend that some good karma apparently bestowed upon me as my protector?

Then, just that suddenly, her breathing stopped, and as I held her hand I found myself whispering, "Go for the light, Mom, go for the light."

The undertaker promised that he would provide two headstones for my parents in the springtime, but I had a strange feeling that I would never be back to see them.

Janet, my mystical soul mate, was not getting any younger, nor was I. She was forty-seven, ten years younger than I was, and I wondered how many more trips we could make. Was that young girl that I met in a laundry room over twenty years ago an enchanted being that would lead me to my destiny?

During the many years we had been together, she had never let me down once. She never questioned our decisions, never complained about how we lived, and now she was walking beside me again with the courage of a lioness and a heart that was as strong and true as ever.

Janet, "After the funeral, we weren't sure what to do, and then our karma intervened once again. A kind nun at the Bhavana Society referred me to a Canadian nun living in Thailand, thinking that I might be interested in going back to Southeast Asia. When I got in touch with the nun, she invited me to join both her and her abbot, along with a few other senior monks, on a trip they were planning to California, Mexico,

171

and Canada. During the trip, I was ordained by Ajahn Lee in Mexico, after which I accompanied the group back to Thailand where I lived at Wat Phratat Foon with the nun, along with Ajahn Luen.

So I was off, with Ed remaining behind again to dispose of our belongings that now included a mobile home. The old Toyota was still running, amazingly, and Ed was able to sell it for about what he originally paid.

He moved in with Bhante G for awhile, and then headed for Thailand himself. He would be at Wat Pah Ban That, two hundred kilometers from where I was staying – far enough away that we would see each other occasionally, but not close enough to interfere with each other's practice or raise eyebrows with the villagers.

I made myself at home again in Thailand, and was soon living out in the jungle with my residence consisting of only a bamboo platform about a foot off the ground with mosquito netting as walls.

This was much more dangerous than living in the huts back at Wat Pah Nanachat years ago, but after training for years, I now had little fear of living in nature, which actually deepened my meditation. I walked for hours back and forth (walking meditation) alongside my little platform that somehow protected me from the cobras that roamed the jungle.

I was also certain that my abbot could read minds. I once tested him by thinking, 'If you can read my mind, walk over here, right now, past where I am standing.' At the time I was standing in an area where it was rare for him to enter, yet only a few minutes later, there he was!

Occasionally the abbot would take us to visit spe-

cial advanced monks at different monasteries in the area. It was always interesting and a treat. One time I visited Ajahn Maha Boowa's monastery where Ed was staying and met the senior monk from the UK, Ajahn Pannavaddho, who at the time had been with Ajahn Maha Boowa for over forty years. Ajahn Pannavaddho and an American monk, Ajahn Silaratano, were instrumental in arranging for Ed's full ordination not long after that.

On one visit, I joined some others having tea with the two monks in an area behind the main hall – just bare jungle floor under some trees with a few small stools. A few other monks had gathered around in the very informal setting, some sitting on the ground.

This was an informal get together every day after the meal at eleven o'clock and a time to ask questions, so I mentioned to him that I wasn't sleeping very well. Ajahn Pannavaddho said that my 'citta' (mind that carries on after death) wasn't relaxed.

I returned to my monastery and after meditating for months and living for weeks out in the jungle on a small platform with only mosquito netting between me and the cobras, I found that I was not only sleeping better, but I was getting control of my sleep as well, to the point where my mind became an alarm clock. I could wake up whenever I told myself I wanted to within minutes!"

One day I was visiting Janet's monastery while her abbot was working with a seriously distressed young village woman. She was possessed with some kind of psychosis and was screaming and thrashing about in the courtyard of the monastery. Her family and other villagers were looking on as the abbot chain smoked cigarettes and calmly talked to her for hours. Finally, the girl curled up on the courtyard pavement and went to sleep, and apparently was never troubled again after the encounter.

In the meantime, I had nestled into Wat Pah Ban That, the home monastery of Ajahn Maha Boowa who was unquestionably the most renowned meditation monk then living in Thailand. I didn't see too much of him as a layperson and never spoke to him personally, but the little I did notice was impressive.

He was about eighty-two at the time and certainly fearless. While I was there, a cancerous tumor was discovered that had invaded the lining of his bowel and began to spread. A battery of doctors were flown in from Bangkok and insisted that he undergo immediate surgery. Instead, and without the slightest concern as if he only had a headache, he opted for some Chinese herbs relying on the power of his meditation to take care of things. He lived for fourteen more years.

After six months at Wat Pah Ban That, I took full ordination as a Buddhist monk with the help of an American monk, Ajahn Silaratano, and the beloved senior English monk, Ajahn Pannyavaddho who has since passed away. When he died, hundreds of monks from over three hundred monasteries throughout Thailand attended his funeral.

After ordination, Ajahn Maha Boowa shipped me off for some basic training to a very strict, isolated 'boot camp' at Wat Pah Daan Wi Weg near Nong Kai just across the Mekong River and Laos. This was great, because Ajahn Maha Boowa's wat was just too busy for me with thousands showing up at the monastery during holidays. Now, however, I was four hundred kilometers from Janet!

Fifteen to twenty monks usually inhabited Wat Pah Daan Wi Weg and fortunately included a fellow American monk who spoke fluid Thai, Cambodian and Laotian. My kuti was deep in the forest, about a half mile from the main hall and situated on the upper end of a massive, flat rock. There were large flat rocks on both sides with deep ravines separating them (havens for cobras), and surrounding everything was dense jungle.

The six by seven foot hut was perched on the customary four stilts with each stilt fitted with a small pan filled with oil to keep out ants, scorpions, and termites. Steps led to a porch at the entrance of the small hut, which had two windows with shutters to protect the occupant from the heavy storms that would soon arrive.

The tin roof looked as if it would hold up well during the rains and was clear of low hanging branches that would invite vipers to drop off trees and become unwelcome guests. Inside on the floor were a lantern and a water jug, and in a corner was a tiny table with a candle and some incense. The solitary adornments on the back wall were a pair of geckos, the ever-present foot long lizards that considered this hut their home as well.

The floor and walls were made of planks cut from large trees by villagers using a two-man saw and manually cutting the twenty-foot logs end-to-end to make boards. This was backbreaking, tedious work for the young village men who would work all day without stopping, except for a few bites of rice and a coke at noon. These impoverished villagers gave up a great deal of their time and resources to support the

175

monks, and I vowed to work as hard as I could to find enlightenment so that I could somehow repay them. Their generosity always astounded me.

A monk's routine in Thailand varied little no matter where he stayed. In the afternoons, I would join the monks at the well near the main hall where we each drew a bucket of cold water for our bath. This bathing area also served as a meeting place where the monks met twice a month to make their brooms for sweeping the paths and to wash and dye their robes by boiling them with the orange bark from the Jackfruit tree.

I would walk back to my hut after the bath and practice meditation for the rest of the evening and usually late into the night. How could I be happier? I had two geckos as companions and my meditation was improving, too. I was beginning to feel at ease with this practice.

While I was there, I was able to work on jhanas, which are the eighth step of the Buddha's Eight Fold Path. These deep states of concentration have the power to shift one's consciousness dramatically, but as one could imagine, I soon found myself lost to the point that I had to write a monk in Australia.

I became acquainted with Ajahn Brahm in Thailand at Wat Pah Nanachat in 1981 just before he shipped out to Australia to develop a monastery there. He had since become well known for his insightful, in-depth instructions regarding jhanas, which can be extremely complicated. When he answered me, his three-page letter was hand printed and spaced with such preciseness that I was positive it was done with a fancy computer font. Upon close examination (under a magnifying glass years later), sure enough, tiny dissimilarities could be seen between the characters. This preciseness was an indication of his careful attention to detail that is so important in advanced meditation practice.

In his letter, he said that it was almost a miracle that my letter ever reached him, and he therefore felt obligated to reward such good karma with a reply! All I knew about Ajahn Brahm at the time was that he went to Australia fifteen years ago, but that's all I knew, so I addressed it to *'Ajahn Brahm, Australia'* because I had no way to get a proper address in the middle of a Thai jungle.

In addition to working on jhanas, there was the everyday routine to follow. A little before sunrise, I would make my way through the night on a narrow trail to the hall, being careful of the Russell Vipers that liked to curl up in the middle of the paths looking very much like little innocent piles of leaves. In the hall, we would all meet and then start walking to the villages nearby to collect our alms, a custom that has been unchanged for twenty five hundred years. At this wat, we didn't meditate as a group; everybody was advanced enough to be on their own.

I fell into a very relaxed routine and my meditation went deeper. Many times at night, just before falling into absorption stages of mediation, beautiful visions of deep color, sometimes only as a color itself but many times appearing as fields of flowers or intricate designs, filled the evenings. Strange words and teachings appeared as well, one after the other and each having many meanings that I couldn't readily understand. It was that same voice that had visited me many times before while in between stages of deep meditation.

Words would appear such as "Be level, true, and correct." "Go deeper in the valley." "The citta (mind) is ahead of the times." "There are seeds to pick about but not talk about." "Think deep, pure thoughts." "There is a great difference between a material void and the immaterial void." "The brain is dead."

These phrases came from out of the blue, as Einstein's Theory of Relativity that he admitted came to him in a flash and had nothing to do with what he was working on. At times, the meanings seemed clear, but as my practice deepened over the years, their meanings would change. Many, many phrases appeared that I didn't record and wished that I had. They were fleeting however; small wisps of consciousness that if not immediately written down would be lost forever like a morning dream, and I chose not to disrupt my meditation by recording them.

The Zen monks at Shasta Abbey regarded all these visions and words as irrelevant 'makyo,' only traps to keep the meditator from going deeper. According to St, John of the Cross, however, authoritative words that arise in meditation can be illuminating.

Therefore, I was torn regarding these phrases that constantly came up. Down deep I knew that in order to experience profound states of concentration or jhanas, I would have to keep my concentration pure and let go of any visions and words that appeared. That involved even the substantial ones strong enough to rise up in my consciousness and become significant including the white lights, the rapture – everything.

These types of experiences indicated to me that much more was going on than my limited physical senses could detect, and to believe that there was nothing out there, except what I could perceive and get my head around, must have been the ultimate conceit. Many regrets came up at Daan Wi Weg as well, a natural enough reaction when the mind begins to go deep. After all, it is the mind's last line of defense before it gives in to stillness.

The forest was abounding in wildlife with barking deer, squirrels, and snakes of all kinds. Consequently, it was a haven for ticks as well. I had to examine my entire body daily for the little rascals that were the size of pinheads because if I missed one, it would grow as big as an eraser head in only a few days and be almost impossible to dislodge. I still have scars from the ones I missed.

Cobras would sun themselves in the ravines between the rock formations that surrounded my kuti, but they behaved themselves and rarely ventured under my kuti as long as I didn't disturb them.

However, I had to be careful when practicing my walking meditation in the forest because they loved to lie in my path. It was a good practice in awareness, and since I was looking through my '*third eye*' in the middle of my forehead most of the time whether meditating or not, it was easy to spot them because the awareness was so uncluttered. Few practicing monks were ever bitten in Thailand.

Gorgeous, purple wild orchids grew in a small area on top of an adjoining rock formation a short distance from my kuti, always tempting my endless desires that constantly looked for the slightest excuse to raise their persistent heads. Getting to the orchids required navigating through the ravines and the cobras, which I gladly risked because I loved meditating in the middle of those flowers. Since the snakes liked the ravines as well, constant disagreements erupted over who had the right of way, but somehow we worked it all out.

One night, about two a.m., I was sitting in meditation when I heard and felt something extremely heavy coming up the steps of my kuti. The whole hut was shaking! My first thought was that it could only be two or three large monks, but they would never interrupt me in the middle of the night. In addition, none of the monks was large!

I listened closely, with my heart in stop mode, but there were no further sounds . . . except for heavy breathing. It was too deep and guttural for human breathing, so whatever kind of non-human it was that came up my steps was now waiting on my porch, and this was really spooky.

I cautiously cracked the door open to have a look. After all, the whole kuti shook like an earthquake when it came up the steps; and what I saw made me quickly close the door and think, *What in the hell is that?*

I had never seen anything like it in my life! It looked like a huge black bear but it had a long, pointed snout! I was completely befuddled, so I quietly closed the door and tried to go back to my meditation. No luck, I just sat there listening until the animal, which apparently had fallen asleep on my porch for awhile, woke up and decided to leave.

The next day I excitedly told my American colleague what happened. After making some inquiries, he explained that an Asian Bear either had wandered onto the grounds, or was turned loose in the monastery for its own protection. He said that bears were extremely rare and never known to approach any of the monks, and certainly never known to climb the stairs of anybody's kuti!

Well, I felt honored! Perhaps the bear was attracted to the great vibes coming out of such an advanced (ha,ha) meditator's kuti and came to keep me company! I was actually looking forward to see if he would return.

That afternoon after sweeping the paths, I noticed a crowd gathering near the sala. I went over to see what the excitement was, and there, lying in a ravine, was my bear with an arrow in his side. It was dying. I walked up to the hunter and got on my knees and with tears streaming down my face, asked, "Why?" He looked at me as if he didn't understand the English word 'why,' which I'm sure he did, and then as if my display of emotionalism was unbecoming a monk, he then waived me off with the back of his hand.

I later asked my fellow American monk what had happened, but he remained mum. I had become so sensitive to the critters in the forest and their love of life that this kind of thing, I felt, was unforgivable. I could no longer kill anything, and yet I felt as if I had killed the bear myself because of my big mouth. I couldn't forgive myself . . . and my doubts began.

Chapter Twelve

12. Ghost Stories

Janet and I would send letters back and forth, but the Thai postal system would take anywhere from three weeks to never to deliver a letter. If I asked her a question, it would take six weeks minimum for her reply to reach me. Keeping this in mind, when Janet wrote that she had to go to a hospital, and then ended up without transportation back to her monastery, I was upset. Her abbot later said that he would have sent a car for her, had he known, but nevertheless I felt that somebody either dropped the ball or was indifferent about a nun's welfare. She had given up everything for me, and I couldn't stand by and let anything unintelligent happen to her.

I was having problems as well. Vitamin C wasn't available so to manage my grain allergies I stayed away from the sticky rice and made up the calories by consuming huge piles of leafy vegetables. Consequently, my bowl would be overflowing with leafy things, but overflowing nevertheless, and when the Ajahn would walk by and look in my bowl, he would admonish me for being greedy. That forced me to either go back to the rice or lose more weight. I kept trying to eat the rice, the only real source of calories, but all the old symptoms would return along with persistent diarrhea. I was miserable. My practice was going nowhere.

This all fell into the realm of doubt that always comes up in training, and if I had it to do all over again, I may have stayed in Thailand, toughed it out and somehow made sure that Janet had received the medical care she required. Her meditation and practice was deepening, and I knew she was willing to die for her quest because she was tough and determined. I had to reflect, however, on what would be a worse tragedy; dying prematurely before she reaches enlightenment, or leaving an incredible, dangerous country that was so conducive to practice.

Janet: "I was willing to sacrifice everything to keep our vow, even if it meant dying here in Thailand, and Ed knew that. It was up to him what we did next."

I have always followed my heart, and my heart told me that it was time to leave Thailand. Was it my heart? Who knows where decisions come from and which ones lead to delusion? Perhaps we can only go as far as our karma permits us.

When we did return to the States, she required an immediate operation, followed by two cancer surgeries and a knee operation down the road. Yet, I'll never know if my decision led Janet away from finding enlightenment in this lifetime, or whether it gave her the time necessary to accomplish it.

We seemed to have interesting karma whenever we decided to leave Thailand, and again it was a problem just like it was sixteen years ago, but this time it wasn't the police in India, it was the banks in Thailand.

The Asian financial crisis was triggered in 1996-1997 while we were there, beginning in Thailand just after we deposited our life savings of $10,000 in the local bank where I was training. The baht (Thai dollar) then plummeted, and farangs, or Westerners, were all suspected of being money speculators, so foreign funds were frozen. We had no idea what was going on until we went to the local bank to withdraw our funds and found a hundred people lined up outside. When we did make it in, the bank told us that it could not release our funds and that we would have to go to their main branch in Bangkok.

We took the overnight train to Bangkok and went to the main branch as soon as it opened. The manager seemed overwhelmed, regarding the financial emergency that was unfolding, and told us that we could only get our money at the local branch, where we originally deposited the money.

After another train ride and another refusal, we headed back to Bangkok once more. This time I decided to get more assertive, forgetting that I was not in first world America! Fortunately, I didn't end up in a Thai prison because a very compassionate Thai manager in the bank was willing to believe us when we said that we had been practicing as a monk and nun in the forest, and that Janet was ill.

After three tense days, the manager was able to verify our religious status and released our money, but we were paid off in bahts, the local currency, and not in the dollars, we initially deposited. After another day of endless paperwork converting the bahts into American Traveler's Checks, we were finally on our way back to Colorado.

Janet: "Ed was really worried, but I was not worried at all. I trusted him completely, as I always had, to get us back home."

A legend in Boulder persists that an old Arapaho

chief, Chief Niwot, put a curse on any white man who dared violate his territory by moving into Boulder. The curse was that people seeing the beauty of this valley would want to stay (and therefore cursed to return time after time). So, true to the curse, back to Boulder we went arriving at the bus station with our piddling life's savings.

Janet was having health issues and we were getting older, two indisputable facts that nudged us to buckle down. We had to figure out what to do when we could no longer support ourselves in old age. We couldn't help but recall a Thai monk who joked about Westerners who still wanted to ordain and live in the monasteries at a very late age. He called them in Thai, "Waste of food!"

Janet: "We worked hard for three years in Boulder and eventually saved enough to buy a small mobile home in a quiet park. We couldn't wait! The apartments we were living in were noisy day and night, in contrast to the mobile home that was peaceful and quiet enough that we could take the next step of our journey. Our concentration had developed to the point where it was time to use it to cut through with 'Investigation' of our body and mind. Now we were going to find out if what the Buddha said was true about what continues in the afterlife."

Are we a wispy soul? The Buddha said no. He said that there was no underlying soul.

Are we annihilated? The Buddha said no again. He said that there was no eternal sleep. That would be too easy!

He claimed that something continues, but not the

fabricated 'self' or personality of our mind. What continues is karma.

Karma is not our names, personalities and fames, but consists entirely of our habit patterns. In modern terminology, these tendencies and actions were as a continuous electrical circuit (karma) that fed light bulbs (our bodies and minds) that would light up for awhile, burn out, and be replaced by another light bulb. This cycle would occur over and over until the light bulbs accumulated enough wisdom not to plug themselves in again and suffer the burn out!

So how would we go about finding out if this is true? The Buddha said that we shouldn't believe anything he says without proving it for ourselves, so where should we begin? We decided to start with our bodies in order to see if a permanent 'self' or soul resides there.

Our investigation revealed animal like things; teeth, skin, fingernails and toenails, body hair and head hair. Were they our beautiful hair and nails? They definitely were not, when a nail clipping dropped on the floor or a hair ended up in the soup – or when a week-old dead animal lay decaying by the side of the road.

Only soft tissue and bones could be found in this body; a temporary physical body that went no further than this bone in our arms. That was the end of it.

And if the bones in our body are removed? What remains is a bucket of slush. And if the water is then removed? What remains is a jar of dust. And when the dust blows away . . . ?

Inside the body, we found squirmy tubes and things. A tube is connected to a bag filled with undigested food leading to bowels and feces, a diaphragm pushes air, a screen strains out poisons, and a pump relentlessly moves blood. We found the body to be as a comfortable house built near a raging river where a flood could wash it away at any moment. Could this fragile, impermanent body be the core of our being; our '*self*?' No.

Does the *self* then reside in the mind? Our investigations revealed four aspects of mind – contact, feeling, memory, and thinking. *Contact* was when a sound touched an ear or a sight touched an eye.

Immediately after this initial contact, the mind quickly decided how it generally *felt* about the contact – pleased, indifferent, or unhappy.

After contact and feeling, *memory* arises. Memory identifies the contact and stores any new additional information.

So there is *contact* with a sense object, how we generally *feel* regarding this contact, and then storing the experience in *memory,* three steps.

The fourth step is *thinking* about all of this and making plans.

Each of these facets of mind arise and pass dependent on each other, so where can an overlying 'self' be found in any one of them standing alone? It can't. They are all merely sense stimulations following each other as tracks follow a cart. Does this mentally fabricated 'self' continue after death? How could it?

Although we intellectually investigated our bodies and minds like this, no insight surfaced. There was, however, something we missed in this investigation. There was an important connection we had to make beyond mind and intellect if our investigation was to deepen into wisdom.

We were able to understand intuitively and experientially that mind and body parts were nothing but arising and passing phenomena with no 'self' behind them, but what did that mean in the grand scope of things?

Then we recalled something that we learned at Shasta Abbey that perfectly fit our investigations, the Three Characteristic of Material Existence – impermanence, no-self, and discontent.

The body and mind parts are subject to change, of course, but we mistakenly identified with them, trying to make them permanent and mistakenly seeing them as our permanent 'self.' They were not ourselves; they were merely arising and passing phenomenon and thus embodied the first and second characteristics – *impermanence* and *no-self*.

With just an imagined control over this body and mind, and no ultimate control, we were trapped with no real power but an imagined responsibility. This, of course, is a recipe for stress, which turns out to be the third characteristic of material existence – *discontent*.

Our investigation revealed that embedded in our body and mind was *impermanence, no self and discontent*. How interesting. More fascinating was the fact that these three characteristics of *impermanence, no self* and *discontent* were a clue to the puzzle, the key to gaining wisdom from our direct, intuitive knowledge of our body and mind.

As this wisdom came to fruition, we eventually found body and mind to be quite innocent, which allowed us to use them without the concern and confusion we had previously experienced when we owned them. It was not necessary to add desire, attachment, and clinging to these aspects of our body and mind, or

189

other bodies and minds for that matter. We could merely allow everything to come and go in life, just as thoughts come and go in meditation.

At this stage, we experienced a burst of energy. We had no interest in bettering our station in life now, and only wanted a quiet place to live where we could both practice and fulfill the responsibilities of taking care of ourselves as we aged.

We went through the motions of life; eating, sleeping, working, and burning off some old karma that still blindsided us occasionally, but it was as if we were just marking time. There was something else that we were destined to do.

Our meditation now had developed to a stage where we simply 'were.' Our life consisted of 'being,' which is difficult to explain because it sounds much like what we did before we ever meditated, but it was light years from that. It mattered little whether we were sitting or doing our daily chores; things happened from a totally engaged, but at the same time disinterested perspective now.

Janet: "With a little money saved and an underlying determination to find whatever was yet undiscovered, we headed for a place where the weather and forests reminded us of Thailand – the Gulf Coast of Florida. Our wisdom was not complete. Restless karma continued to keep us 'going' and 'doing.'

Ed was nearing his sixties now with me only ten years behind, and we had to get serious about how we were going to make it with no support as we entered old age."

Luckily, this was before the housing bubble so we were able to buy a modest house with no down payment or work history – or anything else for that matter. All that was required was a signature and proof that we were breathing! Florida was on fire economically, and in no time, we were making close to $80,000 a year. Did it mean anything to us? Apparently, not much, considering what was coming next.

We continued to earn and save money because we were getting older and had little savings, and we had nobody to back us up. When I wasn't selling cars, which was a quick way to make good money without a resume; and when Janet wasn't selling furniture, we were busy promoting fledgling meditation classes in our home.

Janet: "It's funny how our meditation instilled in both of us a lot of energy and honesty that drew customers to us. It was so easy to help people buy cars and furniture; we didn't have to 'sell' anything at all. Our hearts, however, were really in our little meditation class.

One night at class, we met a couple who mentioned an available fifteen-acre plot in South Florida that the owner might offer for a meditation center. It was an isolated area in the country where we could perhaps establish a meditation group, and who knows – even find a monk to live there. It was just what we were looking for!

The property was fifteen miles out of Naples and although it was located in mosquito-infested swamps, we didn't think that the drive or the mosquitos would discourage anyone. Chalk up lesson number one!

We worked hard on the Naples center, but it was

to no avail. Things didn't work out and we became discouraged. Then, unexpectedly in 2008, our karma took over once again.

The couple that initially suggested the South Florida property now mentioned a Thai meditation temple in Central Florida and suggested we check it out. The temple was established by a very special and highly respected monk – Luang Por – who had temples in both America and Thailand.

So one day we decided, on the spur of the moment, to make the drive from Fort Myers to the Okeechobee, Florida temple and take a look. It sounded innocent enough.

When we arrived, Luang Por was not there. Once the resident monks discovered that we lived in Thailand as a monk and nun, however, we were warmly welcomed. We were also invited to come back in a few weeks to meet Luang Por, who was currently residing at his main temple in Texas, would be in Florida.

It turned out that Luang Por would be there over Memorial Day weekend, unfortunately a busy retail period where we both had to show up for work on Monday. We decided to chance it, however, and make a quick trip to Central Florida to see Luang Por on Sunday, our day off, but we had to get back that afternoon so we could be ready for work the next day."

There were about twenty monks and a hundred or so lay people in the hall when we arrived, so we had no chance to even get close, let alone say hello. He was revered. We just kept our heads down and quietly joined in with the ceremonies, and then lunch."

We were just about to head home when a layman took us aside and said that if we would like to speak to Luang Por, he would arrange it. So, we decided to wait. A few hours later Luang Por was still surrounded by throngs of people all talking Thai, and we had no choice but to head back home. The layman insisted, however, that we should stay – just awhile longer.

Another hour went by and suddenly Luang Por got up, went into his room, and closed the door. Now we had to leave, but the layman caught us and said that Luang Por would be out again shortly, and then for certain we could say hello. His insistence was infectious.

He took us around to a veranda where we waited in ambush, and sure enough, Luang Por came out of a side door. We bowed to him in Thai fashion and as soon as we did his eyes lit up as he said something in Thai to the layman. The layman said that he wanted us to bow in front of some people gathered in a small room so that they could see the correct way of bowing!

After we bowed for the people, Luang Por grinned widely, but an hour or so later, he was still talking in Thai to the gathering crowd. We had no idea what he was saying, but then he said a few words to a laywoman, after which she surprisingly came up to us and said that Luang Por wanted us to join him for lunch the next day!

That was impossible. We had to be at work or we might lose our jobs!

Janet: "But this monk was impressive. He had a straightforward persona about him like many of the advanced forest monks we became acquainted with in Thailand, so we were torn. We got the address where he would be the next day, which was not far from Fort

193

Myers, and then headed home without a commit-ment."

We couldn't sleep. This monk was the real deal, and the fact that we could be fired if we didn't show up for work the next morning didn't help. We couldn't pinpoint how we could spot an authentic monk, but we both felt something very intuitive. The next morning I called both our employers, fibbed a little (bad seafood) and got away with it. Considering what was about to happen, however, I could have saved that little bit of bad lying karma and not called in at all!

The next day after meeting Luang Por for lunch, we all squeezed into a small living room with Luang Por and two of his monks. Only a handful of people were there including the couple that we knew from Naples and a Thai laywoman who served as our inter-preter. Luang Por had his eyes closed with his hands on his knees, palms up, as if he was meditating. The interpreter said that she never saw him do that before.

He opened his eyes and looked at Janet and me. He said that he had been waiting for us for seventeen years, and that he wanted us to take over an eighty-five acre property in Texas to develop a meditation center. Then Luang Por started chewing his Betel Nut. The interpreter whispered to us, "Nobody here knows about these eighty-five acres!"

We were floored, not just because of the unusual vibes we felt in his presence, but because of his di-rectness and non-hesitation with two people that he had only met for a brief time the day before. We didn't know what to say until I finally blurted out, "That means we would have to leave our jobs and sell our home in Fort Myers."

After the interpreter faithfully relayed my message, Luang Por with a big grin said, "Good!"

Janet: "That did it for us. He could have said that we should take time to think it over carefully because it was a big decision, blah, blah, blah, but he already knew how this was all going to come out. He knew as well that our frantic life in Fort Myers trying to make money and secure ourselves was not conducive to our practice. He was giving us a way out."

This was coincidentally all happening just as the housing market peaked and was now heading south. Our realtor warned us that it would take months or longer, maybe years to sell even at the modest price we were asking, but regardless, we slowly started giving things away . . . again.

Three days later, however, we had two offers on the house and sold it immediately! The realtor was floored, and when we told her the story about Luang Por, she actually broke down into tears and said it was a miracle! And maybe it was. Later we told Luang Por about selling our house in three days. He just smiled.

It was time to leave the Sunshine State. We packed a few things in our Toyota Corolla, and with shovels and rakes hanging off the sides, headed for the great state of Texas.

After staying at the main temple in Texas for awhile, Luang Por, along with a van full of laypeople and monks, took us to visit the property. The trip began with eighty miles on the I-10, then a double lane highway for forty-five miles, followed by a scary thirteen-mile curvy ranch road on high cliffs through the

195

hill country before dropping into five miles of dirt roads, creek crossings, cattle guards, and bump gates.

We doubted if even dirt bikers would take a chance on this one! This was really isolated, with the nearest full-time neighbors almost three miles away from the property. There was no traffic or human life to be seen anywhere! And of course it was out of range of any cell phones.

Janet: "I could not believe it! This was so remote and so beautiful with large oaks below and small cedar trees all over the hills. We could see seven 'mountains' from the base of the property and felt as if we were in a miniature Colorado.

However, there were rocks all over the place and hard to walk on and I knew that I would have to make some paths someday. Also the big creek bed was cleared of trees, which I could not figure out at the time. I guess I didn't notice the 'flash flood' signs back then, and didn't realize how trees in creek beds can back flood waters into your house!"

We returned to the main temple after our initial peek at the property and settled in. One day I naively asked Luang Por if our Corolla was adequate, prompting a one-word reply, "No!"

"What should I get?" I asked.

His interpreter said, "A Chevy pickup."

"What kind?" I asked.

"A four wheel drive V-8 with a heavy duty suspension."

After a trip to the local Chevy dealer the next day, our Corolla was just a fond memory and we were sporting a brand new Silverado!

Luang Por wouldn't allow us to return again to the property, not just yet, and had us stay at a branch temple for awhile. After pestering him for weeks to let us get started on the center, he finally gave in and said we could visit, but we couldn't stay overnight. For the life of me, I could not figure this out. Why wouldn't he allow us to live on the property, after all this is what we gave everything up to do!

Only years later after spending many seasons out there where the temperature can get down to eight degrees Fahrenheit, did we appreciate his wisdom. We would have been faced with frozen water pipes, no heaters, and no help! Luang Por never explained why he did what he did, and many times, we wondered why he did things that we disagreed with. It was only in retrospect that we were able to catch on to his wisdom.

It was still winter and getting dark early, so most days we would leave the branch temple at four a.m., arrive at the center by seven a.m. and work until it got dark around five p.m. After a few months, Luang Por relented and allowed us to stay overnight. That gave more hours to work! Our energy was unlimited.

Janet: "One thing that struck me was there were no animals around, but that would change."

The land was previously owned by a Thai couple. The husband was very sick, close to dying when they went to see Luang Por, who had a gift of healing since he was in his early twenties as a young monk, but he kept his gift under wraps because that kind of publicity has drawbacks.

The man was able to recover from his illness and

in gratitude; the couple donated their land to Luang Por with hopes that the property would be used for meditation someday.

The land had the basics, a good electrical line strung along the meadow for about half a mile, and a deep, pure well. The two-tank septic system that was dynamited out of the solid rock was an added plus, however, there was no phone on the property.

We talked to the telephone company about a phone line and were surprised that they had a line already going along the dirt road, which meant that all they had to do was extend the line to the main building on the property. However, that involved about six hundred feet of trenching through many rocks.

Luang Por wanted to visit, and we were hoping to have a phone installed before he came out, but after waiting for weeks the phone company still did not schedule our installation. Strangely enough, as we approached the property with Luang Por on the day he decided to visit, we were shocked to see the phone company with a huge circular trencher tipped with carbide teeth chipping through the rocks from the road toward the meditation hall.

Luang Por took it all in and within minutes summoned his main monk. The monk then asked the telephone supervisor if we could hire them to dig a trench from the well down to the main buildings so that we could bury the water lines and not have to drain them in freezing weather. The well sat two hundred feet up on the hill, so I figured that they were too busy to do such a thing, but I didn't understand the persuasive powers of Luang Por yet! And of course they said they would. It was a strange thing how quickly Luang Por could assess things and make snap decisions, and how people would follow him.

After the phone line was buried and the phone hooked up, the workers started on the waterline trench. The shelf rock on the hill was almost impenetrable, requiring two changes of carbide bits while trying to dig the trench. Three days later while they were finishing, I stuck ten hundred dollar bills in my pocket, hoping it was enough, and asked the two men, now covered in rock dust, how much we owed them.

The boss looked at his partner, then looked back at me and said, "Would a hundred be okay?" It was close to Christmas and I knew they had kids, so I gave them each two hundred, launching a close bond between these big-hearted telephone linemen and the 'Buddhists.' Never did we have a lightning strike or outage where they weren't out the next day, traveling miles on the dirt back roads in all kinds of weather to get to us.

And so the work began. While Janet was busy clearing and burning brush, as well as clearing cabin paths and lining them with rocks, I was building small seven feet by seven feet cabins for guests.

Janet: "Ed was the builder – I was the landscaper! Making meditation paths and burning wood were my favorite jobs, as well as hand feeding the black squirrels and deer that began visiting the property. They were so trusting. Our first black squirrel arrived after months of no animals around, and we named her Eight Ball. It was the first black squirrel that I had ever seen in my life!"

We soon made another great discovery out there –

ghosts! Apache Indians had lived on the land for generations, and they were still around, at least in spirit! One guest, who subsequently ordained and is now a monk in Thailand, saw a long black haired man in strange clothing one night standing at the entrance of his cabin for a moment, looking straight at him. This had to be a ghost. Nobody would ever happen to just drop by out there in the boondocks, and the cabins were hidden up in the hills. Even people who knew where the property was couldn't find it!

One afternoon, shortly after we began living on the property, I was gutting an old travel trailer by removing the appliances so I could remodel it. I would remove a screw, set the drill down for a few seconds, and then remove the next screw. Right in the middle of this sequence I reached for my drill and it was gone! I knew I couldn't have misplaced it because I was just using it a second ago! This was strange. Was my mind going? I looked all over the trailer and then happened to look outside. There it was in the middle of the deck! I did not put it there.

A senior monk was laying tile alone in the bathroom one night, smoking a cigar. When he looked up, standing in front of him was an Indian in full headdress watching him work! The monk was not alarmed at all and simply offered the Indian the cigar, but as soon as he did, the Indian disappeared.

One day Luang Por was visiting. He was sitting with Janet and I on the deck but he had his back turned to us and seemed to be talking to someone out toward the meadows and then up in the sky, moving his arms in an animated conversation. When I went closer, however, there was nobody there, just Luang Por.

Janet: "I am convinced that Luang Por could read minds. A group of us, with Luang Por leading, walked up to our flag that flew on top of the highest hill. When we reached the top, I was thinking how nice it would be to live up here in a cabin, but then realized it wouldn't be practical. Then I thought just sleeping up here would be nice.

Just after I had this thought, Luang Por mentioned something to one of his monks, and then the monk came over to me and translated what he said, "Tell her to bring her sleeping bag up here!"

One night two laywomen were sleeping in the main hall. The first woman shook the second one awake and said that there were small lights circling around. The second woman wasn't sure what the other woman was referring to and thought it might be fireflies or something that got into the room, but when she actually looked, she said it was supernatural. She called them 'devas.'

Janet, "One night I was in my cabin and just finished meditating. It was dark and all the blinds were down except for the nearest one that was halfway up. I looked out the window and saw a bright light, like a flashlight, coming up the main path a hundred feet away. It was flashing in and out through the branches. At the time, only Ed and I were at the property and Ed was in his cabin a quarter mile away. He would never come to my cabin. If it were an emergency, he would call me on our walkie-talkies first.

Although I knew it couldn't be Ed, for some reason I was not afraid even though it might have been a

201

stranger, but how would anyone find the property, let alone my cabin, in the dark? As it got closer, it turned off the main path and started toward my cabin. This is when I saw many lights, maybe two dozen blinking on and off. They couldn't be lightning bugs because they were in a pattern, all hovering about five feet above the path and moving closer to my front porch. I didn't know what they were.

I wasn't worried and sat there relaxed. Something then told me to open the front blind and I got up just in time to see the pattern of lights right in front of my cabin starting to go straight up into the sky, until they were all gone."

The first five years were spent building cabins and setting up a teaching center. We would make the one hundred and sixty mile round trip into town every two weeks for food and supplies, and often make the two hundred and eighty mile round trip to the main temple to see Luang Por and our supporters. We learned fast to double check our lists because there was nothing worse than arriving back at the property and forgetting something at Home Depot that would hold you up for two more weeks!

We set up a website and did what we could to let people know we were there, but the logistics were against us. It was a three-hundred mile round trip to an airport, and the property was rather dangerous, as Texas ranches are, with rattlesnakes and flash floods. It would have taken 911 close to an hour to get to the property from the nearest small town, and then another hour and half to get to a hospital.

Helicopters were not much better because a paramedic would have to call them in, which means the paramedic would have to drive to the property first. A chopper could cost from $15,000 to $30,000 a trip, so we were careful of rattlesnakes, but we came very close a few times.

The closest near bite was when a big diamond back was coiled two feet from my leg. I was usually very mindful because rattlers are hard to see among the rocks, but for some reason I was busy looking through the junk pile for a piece of one-inch PVC water pipe and didn't see it. I just heard a buzzing sound. I thought maybe there were some locusts around. I looked up in the trees . . . and then I looked down.

I never wore boots, just sandals or low top sneakers, and when I saw him so close and coiled ready to strike, my first inclination was to stand dead still. I noticed I wasn't scared; I don't think my heart rate even increased – probably a result of meditation and cheating the grim reaper quite a few times, but I couldn't stand there all day. I started backing up real slow until I got out of the magic eight foot circle, and then the rattler and I went our separate ways. I was amazed it never struck me, and I thanked the snake for that, but I couldn't let it hang out near the buildings.

Usually Janet would help with the snakes, but I didn't know where she was. By the time I ran to the tool shed, grabbed my rattlesnake snare and ran back, it was gone. I sat there for awhile looking for it, and sure enough eventually saw it moving twenty feet away under the Juniper/cedar scrub trees. I crawled on my belly to get under the scratchy branches, making sure I didn't get too close but knowing that I had a good six foot reach with my snare. It took awhile, but my rattler finally made a wrong move and put its head right in my snare. He was now on his way to the far end of the property.

Janet: "When we found a rattlesnake, I would keep an eye on it until Ed ran and got our 'snake kit,' consisting of a long-poled snare and a large trash barrel with a burlap bag tied inside. Ed would catch the rattler while I held the trashcan from falling over. Then the hard part, taking it to the furthest reaches of the property and releasing it, and hoping it couldn't find its way back.

Thank goodness I had become accustomed to deadly snakes in Thailand and could now face them without running!"

Flash floods could come at any time. They roar like a freight train taking down everything in their path. The back roads had many signs with markers so that a driver could see how many feet of water were above the roadway. Many roads in the backcountry were nothing more than dry creek beds, including ours, and when the floods came, the roads turned into rivers six feet to fifteen feet deep and fifty to a hundred feet wide. In the narrow areas, it was not unusual to have debris from a flood stacked twenty feet high on some banks.

We experienced a few floods. They usually came in the spring; however, the flood in the fall of 2018 was the worst, competing with the 1955 flood where twenty-six inches of rain fell in a twenty-four hour period.

A flood would completely close the dirt road to the property with the sudden wall of water digging deep crevices and rolling large boulders and logs onto the road, necessitating the county to come out and clear it with heavy equipment. This usually took a week or two, maybe longer depending on how widespread the damage was and considering the sparse county road crews. The 2018 flood closed the five-mile dirt road for weeks.

In the meantime, the only way out would be to walk the two miles to the next dirt road, that would be more or less destroyed as well. Even the paved road, five miles away, would be washed out at times, necessitating a thirty-mile walk to the nearest small town.

So we made sure we had a month's supply of food at all times – mason jars full of honey, rice, powdered milk, and oatmeal, along with canned goods.

Shopping every two weeks involved a daylong trip with over a dozen different stops, meaning that during the winter we would come home after dark. This made the numerous flat tires from sharp rocks an especially troublesome bother, so after living on the property full time for about six years, we had our eyes out for a place to sleep over when we went into town.

By chance, we ran across a mobile home for sale in a quiet senior community located in our shopping town that had medical facilities and a hospital, and about two hours from the property. The owner was almost giving the home away, so we bought it.

Not long after that, Janet had a situation requiring surgery and radiation tying us up for four months. We were fortunate we had the trailer in town and didn't have to make the one-hundred-sixty mile round trip every day from the property for the five weeks of radiation, plus all the doctor appointments. Two years later, she needed a knee operation as well. It's funny how we had the urge to get that trailer. We always preferred living in small cabins or trailers; houses always seemed more than this 'monk and nun' needed.

The time in Texas went fast, as it tends to do when people get older – just a blur. A wink and ten years had gone by. The property still only averages about one car a day down the dirt road, if that, and we have lost some neighbors while other neighbors remain, always watching our backs. Yet the rocks and trees probably haven't noticed the passage of time at all.

Not too many people visit the property anymore. Perhaps if we would have been better teachers things might have worked out differently, but we did the best we could, and we can't ask for more than that of others or ourselves. We were always well supported by the laypeople.

Luang Por is retired and living in Thailand now. He visits the States once a year for a few weeks and occasionally still takes time to visit the property. We are retired as well from teaching meditation but still honor our promise to Luang Por to take care of the property for as long as he will have us, and as long as we can make it out there.

We began this journey in a little laundry room forty years ago, and when the Buddha said that life passes as quickly as a flash of lightning, he was on to something. The Buddha never stayed in one place too long either, and again he was spot on. Our greatest insights over the years seemed to come when we were between stops and letting go of everything, and not so much when we were settled down and secure. It's so easy to attach to people and places, and whenever we did that, we invariably fell sound asleep.

So, how does one measure one's life? I'm afraid in

the eyes of the world we are abject failures. We could have accumulated the bank accounts and the offspring that society fancies, but when we met those forks in the road, we, for some reason, went a different way. Being broke or alone never frightened us much, and although we always minimally provided for ourselves and relied on each other for companionship in our journey, we were always more than ready to abandon even these. Two specks of dust in the wind don't generate too much drama.

Thank you for allowing us to share our journey with you. Will our *endless journey* continue? The omniverse is an endless place . . . stay tuned.

E. Raymond and Janet V. Rock's combined eighty-years of meditation experience include two stopovers in Thailand where they practiced in the remote Northeast forests as an ordained Theravada Buddhist monk and nun with Ajahn Chah, Ajahn Maha Boowa, Ajahn Tui, Ajahn Luen and Ajahn Lee. They were also postulants at Shasta Abbey, a Zen Buddhist monastery in northern California under Roshi Kennett, and Theravada Buddhist anagarikas at Amaravati Monastery in the UK and Bodhinyanarama Monastery in New Zealand, both under Ajahn Sumedho.

The authors have meditated with the Korean Master Sueng Sahn Sunim, with Bhante Gunaratana at the Bhavana Society in West Virginia, and with the Tibetan Master Trungpa Rinpoche in Boulder, Colorado. They have also practiced at the Insight Meditation Society in Barre, Massachusetts and the Zen Center in San Francisco.

38345513R00127

Printed in Poland
by Amazon Fulfillment
Poland Sp. z o.o., Wrocław